AN ARCHITECTURE FOR PEOPLE
THE COMPLETE WORKS OF HASSAN FATHY

JAMES STEELE

AN ARCHITECTURE FOR PEOPLE

THE COMPLETE WORKS OF HASSAN FATHY

WHITNEY LIBRARY OF DESIGN
AN IMPRINT OF WATSON-GUPTILL PUBLICATIONS/NEW YORK

Title page *Suq* (covered market) at New Gourna, 1947

Below Hassan Fathy at his home and site office in New Gourna, mid-1940s

Note The spelling of Arabic words has been rendered as consistently as possible; certain exceptions have been made in the case of people or places whose names have become better known in other forms outside Egypt.

Contents

Introduction

Hassan Fathy was born in 1900 in Alexandria to a Sa'idi father and a Turkish mother. It was a middle-class household; his father had risen from a poor background, becoming a landowner and a farmer. From the age of six to early adulthood, Fathy attended British schools in Cairo. He began studying agriculture but switched to architecture and attended the University of Cairo, graduating in 1926.

His work reflects a complex duality of eastern and western influences, and the contradiction between them. On the one hand, Fathy respected and admired European traditions and on the other he resented them as part of a colonial legacy that had threatened Egypt's identity. Fathy was at first eager to emulate a culture that his education had presented to him as superior, and his early work reflects this. He later turned against that culture to invent a style that he believed incorporated the essence of his own heritage.

The issue of Westernism in Fathy's architecture is controversial, given the standing that Fathy has achieved both in the West and the East. Edward Said has identified the phenomenon of 'orientalism' — the Western objectification of countries defined as the Orient in order to facilitate colonial control. This superficial view of the East, incorporating negative elements that imply inferiority, has complex origins, but one strand is the dichotomy between the industrialized West and the non-industrial East, which was the bedrock of the view that Eastern culture lacked the overall organization or motivation necessary to embrace 'progress'.

Like his contemporaries, Fathy was inevitably affected by the mythology of orientalism, while also rebelling against it, and his work reflects both the duality and the self-consciousness of this. At one extreme, his designs can be said to incorporate the view of an easterner looking at his own culture through western eyes and interpreting it as he thought an easterner should.

Egypt has had a particularly unhappy history of foreign occupation and colonial exploitation, and is a model of the negative effects of prolonged cultural confusion among its neighbours. That confusion is not recent, having started with countless foreign invasions

Above right Hassan Fathy

Below right Fathy's family home in Cairo, a traditional house with many features found in medieval buildings in the city. Fathy was influenced by medieval Cairene architecture both aesthetically and for the practical benefits of traditional methods.

Below left The entrance to Fathy's own house in New Gourna, the community project which established his reputation in the 1940s.

Above left Fathy's house in New Gourna. The arrangement of courtyards and terraces is a characteristic concern: they always demonstrate an ingenious use of space while preserving the division between public and private areas.

Fathy on the roof of his house in Cairo, probably 1980s. In the background is the Sultan Hasan Mosque, which inspired his study 'Mosque Architecture' (unpublished manuscript).

Constantinople, asking for Isma'il's deposition, which followed one year later in 1879. Both England and France were then in virtual joint control of the government, in spite of the succession of Isma'il's son Tewfik to power. The major portion of Egypt's national revenue was then diverted to paying back its foreign debts and it was only allowed to retain the amount necessary for administrative expenses. In the face of growing rumours of revolution, a joint force of British and French battleships was dispatched to Alexandria, and defences were put up by the Egyptian army to protect the city. Riots broke out there on 11 June 1882, in which many members of the foreign community were killed or wounded. The French fleet, which was advised by its government not to become involved in any further military action in Egypt, sailed away toward the Suez Canal, while the British answered with bombardment and the occupation of the city. The ultimate result of the occupation of Alexandria was a declaration of war by the Egyptian cabinet, and a final confrontation with Arabia's forces at the village of Tel-al-Kabir, which is halfway between Isma'ilia and Zagazig, on 13 September 1882, followed by British occupation of Cairo the next day.

The British were to remain in Egypt for the next 70 years, through two world wars and nationalistic uprisings within the country. Colonial occupation contributed important institutions, and resulted in the founding of a Khedival library by Ali Pasha Mubarak, as well as the Royal Geographical Society in 1875, and the building of the first zoological garden in Cairo soon afterwards. In his desire to emulate Europe, the Khedive Isma'il encouraged the establishment of newspapers, leading to the founding of the Wadi al-Nil in 1866,

throughout history, and ending only with the takeover of the Government by the Free Officers on 22 July 1952, led by Gamal Abd al-Nasser.

In the thirteen short years between the accession of Isma'il Pasha in 1863 and a declaration of national bankruptcy in 1876, the public debt of Egypt had increased by three hundred per cent. England had extended more than half of this amount, with France providing almost as much. An international commission of enquiry convened two years later in 1878 ultimately led to a joint petition of both powers to the Suzerain in among others. Once such public forums became available, the expression of divisive opinions was not far behind, and it was a journalist named Salim al-Naqqash, rather than a member of the royal family or the government, who first gave the rising tide of nationalism a slogan in print:'Egypt for the Egyptians!' Not long afterwards, more fuel was added to nationalist feelings by Jamal al-Din al-Afghani, who began preaching about the need for religious reform throughout the Middle East. He found an apt disciple named Muhammad Abduh in Egypt, who later established a sizable power base for himself at al-Azhar University. This new religious and nationalistic fervour soon began to have a noticeable impact upon the literature and poetry of the Khedival period, leading to the translation of old texts, and a new style of poetry that was patterned after that of early Islam. With the opening of the Royal Opera House in 1869, which corresponded with the opening of the Suez Canal, a new era in this intellectual renaissance began. Plays such as those put on by the Syrian company of Abu Khalil al-Qabbani began to be given in Cairo, and continued throughout the reign of the Khedive Isma'il. By 1898, nearly two hundred newspapers and journals were being published, including *Al-Ahram* and *Al-Muqattam*, and many of these included poetry, prose and articles, as well as reviews of cultural events. Literature and the theatre flourished.

Several leaders, who had either a direct or indirect influence upon Hassan Fathy during the early years of his architectural development, began to emerge in this fertile intellectual atmosphere. One of these was Taha Husayn, who first attended al-Azhar University for twelve years before entering Cairo University in 1912,

finally going on to the Sorbonne in Paris. His teaching of Ancient History at Cairo University after his return to Egypt in 1919, and the publication of his survey of philosophy called *Qadat al-Fikr*, soon afterwards, both contrasted eastern and western values in a way that had a great impact upon his contemporaries. Husayn has crystallized the outrage that Egyptians felt at the inequities caused by colonial occupation, also embedded in Fathy's architectural campaign:

> Our patriotic duty is to make Egyptians feel – individually and collectively – that God has created them for honour, not for abasement; for power, not for weakness; for mastery, not for quiescence; for distinction, not for obscurity. We must erase from the hearts of Egyptians, individually and collectively, the criminal, the abominable misconception which causes them to imagine that they have been created of a different clay from that of the Europeans, have been compounded of different temperaments from that of Europeans, have been given different minds from those of Europeans.[1]

The Nobel Prize-winning author Naguib Mahfouz, who is also a product of this intellectual renaissance, was born in 1911, and graduated from Cairo University in 1934, eight years after Fathy, with a degree in philosophy. Inspired by the wave of excitement that swept Egypt, as well as the rest of the world, when the tomb of King Tutankhamun was discovered in Luxor, Mahfouz wrote the first of fifty novels based on Pharaonic themes in 1939, called *The Struggle of Thebes*. Based on the Hyksos invasion of ancient Egypt, it was

Fathy's reputation in Egypt was made by the 1940s, but he was the subject of controversy. Modernist factions in academia tried to marginalize him after his initial successes. Since his death in 1989 his influence has been felt internationally, through his pupils and exponents of his approach, in pursuit of sustainable methods and the responsible use of natural materials.

to establish his early pattern of using thinly veiled allegory as a means of political commentary on the British occupation of his country. His writing echoes Fathy's belief that Egypt cannot be built on technology alone, and that all future progress must be tempered with faith and social values.

Hamed Said, an artist who was Fathy's close friend as well as a client, vividly recalls what he has described as the sense of impending catastrophe that prevailed within this intellectual circle in Egypt just prior to the Second World War. He has noted that the main subject of conversation at that time was what was perceived to be a cultural crisis, and a general decline in the level of civilization within the country. He cites this feeling of crisis as the main reason behind the search for cultural identity that characterizes Fathy's work at this time. The general mood of social malaise and overall conviction that something was drastically wrong with the contemporary Egyptian lifestyle led Said to search for his own roots in the past, and he attributes the long period of peace and prosperity of the ancient civilization of his country to its natural, agrarian basis.

The emerging ideals of the Modern movement in Europe in the early part of the twentieth century were diametrically opposed to the preservation of such traditions, producing manifestos that proclaimed a 'New Era'. As Le Corbusier proclaimed in his *Towards a New Architecture* in 1927, the use of materials such as plate glass, steel and reinforced concrete, as well as the images of the industrial age, were to be the basis of the revolutionary changes that he proposed. For him, and many others in this movement, the spaces that could be created by using such technological advances had socially corrective potential, and honesty of expression in the use of this technology was deemed to be an essential prerequisite to a brighter future.

Rather than believing that people could be behaviourally conditioned by architectural space, Fathy felt that human beings, nature and architecture should coexist in harmonious balance. For him, architecture was a communal art, that should reflect the personal habits and traditions of a community rather than reforming or eradicating them. While he was certainly not opposed to innovation, he felt that technology should be subservient to social values, and appropriate to popular needs. His book *Architecture for the Poor*, a call for the integration of nature and industry, prefigures the current ethos of sustainability:

We must find a solution to the hitherto insoluble problem of the clash between the products of industry and the demands of nature and of society. It would be useful to subject technology to the economy and materials of a particular region. In this way the quality and values inherent in the traditional and human response to the environment might be preserved without a loss of the advances of science. Science can be applied to various aspects of our work, while it is at the same time subordinated to philosophy, faith and spirituality.[2]

In an interview with Yorick Blumenfeld, for example, that was published in the *Architectural Association Quarterly* in 1974 under the title 'Beyond the Human Scale,' he said that: 'Arab architecture begins with the interior and goes to the exterior. The function of the space is primary. The outer form must express the forces on the inside.' This statement may seem to place him in the functionalist camp, and yet, in the same interview, he went on to say that 'Space has its own logic. Islamic architecture is one of space and not walls… We are in need of an era of non-functionalism. We are in need of quality with a human touch.'[3]

Intellectual activity in Cairo, at the time that Fathy began his career in the 1920s and 1930s, showed a deep nostalgia for the past, as well as a desire for change, and these inform his work. Several major themes constantly recur. The first of these concerns seclusion and protection of the family, and the issue of privacy, which is a basic requirement in Islamic society, and is particularly important in residential architecture, where the worlds of the family and the guest are defined.

By making this an important priority in each design parti, Fathy was able to establish a finite organizational method in his work, yet also to retain great creative freedom.

The second theme has been called his 'thesis of space' by one of his better-known followers. Fathy created a series of typologies by studying the history of Islamic architecture in general, and the medieval quarter of his own city of Cairo in particular. His conversion of these visible spatial models into a set of rules led to the development of many of the early designs. He especially noted that the internal courtyard, which has been used throughout the Middle East for millennia, had efficiently served as a temperature regulator in each of houses that he studied, and also helped to filter the dust from the air in the city.

In addition to the courtyard, he noted that other spaces, such as the *qa'a*, the main reception room of a house, had adjusted to various cultural changes within a relatively short period of time. In the Cairene house, particularly in both the Mamluk and Ottoman periods, the *qa'a* is a classical example of a traditional archetype. Beginning as an open courtyard flanked by opposing T-shaped *iwans* (alcoves), the *qa'a* came to Egypt from Iraq in the twelfth century, inside the tightly compressed houses of Fustat. In Fustat, the position of the open courtyard remains central, but the T-shaped spaces on either side became more simplified in response to urban conditions. In the course of this change, a fountain was also added to cool the air coming into the courtyard. In its final form, in Fatimid Cairo, the *qa'a* became completely internalized as a result of the increased density and noise of the city. The flanking *iwans*, which eventually dropped the cross-bar of the 'T' to become a simple alcove on each side of the higher covered central court, ultimately created an integral, unified architectural component that was perfectly suited to the social needs of the emerging merchant class of Cairo. As adapted by Fathy, the *qa'a* took on a new significance as a formal residential reception area, as he carefully began to scale down the high central tower of the Mamluk and Ottoman houses to allow it to fit contemporary domestic needs.

The courtyard and the *qa'a* are only two of many such typologies that were adapted by the architect. Fathy did not restrict his historical research to the Fatimid, Mamluk and Ottoman periods alone, but was also interested in the Pharaonic period as well, which serves as a third major theme here. Gouaches of New Gourna and a Pharaonic garden that he has mysteriously entitled *The Parliament of the Pharaohs*, hint at the full extent of that interest, as does his use of ancient Egyptian artistic conventions in several others. In those that use these conventions, walls and gardens as well as walkways and pools are shown in plan and elevation at the same time, just as the figures and scenes in the wall paintings at Luxor and Thebes are shown both from the front and side to assist the viewer in a total understanding of the work. Fathy is known to have been greatly impressed by the research of the archaeologist R. A. Schwaller de Lubicz, whom he met in Luxor while the New Gourna project was under construction. De Lubicz's *The Temple in Man* is an overwhelming work on Pharaonic mathematics and astrology, which traces its relationship to the monumental architecture and art of ancient Egypt.

Fathy attempted to widen the historical content of his architecture beyond the more recent past to the

Alaa al-Din Mustafa, Fathy's Nubian master mason, with whom he worked for much of his career. The lessons taught by Nubian masons – how to build inexpensively using traditional mud-brick vaults and domes – shaped Fathy's architecture.

earliest beginnings of civilization in his country, which today represents an extraordinary layering of historical influences. The Pharaonic age, which began in 3100 BC with the Archaic period, through the Old, First and Intermediate, Middle, Second Intermediate and New Kingdoms, and then on into the Late period, lasted for nearly three thousand years, until the conquest of Egypt by Alexander the Great. Such a relatively long and culturally productive period could certainly not be ignored by an architect with such wide-ranging interests. While intellectually stimulated by the monumental achievements of the Pharaonic period, Fathy was more directly influenced by the vernacular architecture of the Nubians, which opened up a whole new world of possibilities for him.

Once convinced of the long history, durability and cultural applicability of mud brick, as well as its low cost and environmental advantages, Fathy saw no reason why it should not be used on a wider scale. What he could not possibly foresee was the extent of the resistance which arose because of the associations between mud brick and poverty in the mind of the public.

Another theme that emerges is that of the need for architecture to join rather than separate people from the natural world. This belief in the need for unity with nature is convincingly conveyed in Fathy's graphic communication of his architectural intentions in each of these projects, in which nature – what he has called the 'God-made environment' – is given equal status with his sensitivity to it. Such efforts characterize all of his work at all levels, as can be seen in the similarities of approach in an early, modest proposal for a rural farm and the al-Sabah house, which is one of his last works.

From beginning to end, he uses natural ventilation, orientation and local materials, traditional construction methods and energy-conserving techniques.

These efforts probably reached their most refined expression in his design for the village of Baris, which is located in the Kharga Oasis, in the central desert of Egypt. Unlike New Gourna, Fathy's best-known community project, Baris had to fit an as yet undetermined agrarian population and was to be located in an environment that was far more hostile than that of Luxor. The *suq* (open-air market), which was the only part of the village to be completed before construction was cut short by war in 1967, demonstrates Fathy's skills of environmental regulation at their best. Intended as the central distribution area for an isolated agricultural community, this large market complex had to provide cold storage for the perishables that were to be kept there prior to shipment and sale, without any possibility of using air-conditioning. The architect carried out detailed studies of temperature and wind patterns in the area, and of traditional architectural responses to this harsh environment made by local villages nearby. The *suq* was oriented to maximize air movement into it, while higher parts of the building were positioned in such a way as to shade lower areas, to minimize solar gain. Air scoops were designed to reach high up to catch the desert winds and funnel them down through a series of angled baffles that increased the velocity of the air on its way to the basement level where the fruits and vegetables, that were grown in the Oasis itself, were stored. This design shows that the application of scientific knowledge need not be dehumanizing, and that 'technology with a human face' can actually exist.

A further theme that characterizes the work seen here is Fathy's use of aesthetics, harmony and proportion. As an accomplished violinist as well as an architect, Fathy was receptive to the compositional potential of musical harmonics in his work and constantly mentions this in his writings. Since music is the most intuitive, and least visual of all the arts, his exposure to it helped to develop this ability within him, which carried over into his architecture. The sense of rhythm and pattern that typifies the projects shown here also reveals the fine hand of a musician, which is especially evident in the composition of the site plan of New Gourna, and the proposal for the Harraniya weaving village, and even more in the rendering of the Isma'il Abd al-Razik resthouse, or the elevation of the Riad house. In each of these, his graphic communication of forms most nearly suggests musical notation. His blending of intuitive musical skills, with his growing interest in the mathematical relationships used in the ancient Egyptian canon of measurement, has been introduced here in relation to several of his projects, and deserves further study, as it was obviously a major factor in his design methodology. No analytical system, however, should be credited with producing what are, finally, extremely sensitive expressions of the highest sensibilities of the human spirit.

There may be said to be six general principles which guided Hassan Fathy throughout his career: his belief in the primacy of human values in architecture; the importance of a universal rather than a limited approach; the use of appropriate technology; the need for socially oriented, co-operative construction techniques; the essential role of tradition; and the re-establishment of national cultural pride through the act of building.

The first of these principles, Fathy's fundamental humanism, has anticipated many concerns about the destruction of the environment that are being voiced with increasing urgency today. He set himself apart from the majority of practitioners of his time by rejecting the temptation to reduce the users of buildings to anonymous ciphers, and he was able to proclaim proudly the vital importance of each individual regardless of social or economic status.

In his design for the village of New Gourna, he astonished critics with his insistence on the custom design of each house in a settlement intended for seven thousand people. When this level of concern is contrasted with other approaches taken toward housing at this time, such as Le Corbusier's Unité d'Habitation in Marseilles, France, it becomes very obvious where

Fathy's sympathies lie. The New Gourna project identified him with a deep concern for the plight of the homeless throughout the world. He not only sought to help the poor of his own country, but also saw his thesis as being applicable throughout the world.

Fathy was not limited by a narrow functional or technical view of architecture, but saw it instead as an art that involved every aspect of human endeavour. This second principle, that of universality, shows a keen awareness of the implications on his work of theology, philosophy, history, sociology, science and physics, as well as music, literature, art and dance. He consistently dealt with all the influences on his work in a non-judgmental way. In searching for the sources of Islamic architecture, for instance, he did not limit himself within national borders, but had a wider perspective. While the material he chose and the spaces he evolved had deep spiritual, psychological and cultural associations within his own country, they also have the power to evoke a much wider response.

In his conversations and writings, he was capable of a wide range of reference, from Lao Tze, Dante Aligheri and Antoine de Saint Exupéry, whose *Citadelle* was a constant source of delight to him; to Rabindranath Tagore, Jacques Berque and Schwaller de Lubicz. His personal library reflected his universal interests, including such diverse works as *Le Monde des Symboles* produced by Les Presses Monastiques and *Camaanes du Roi Amaury Premier de Jerusalem en Egypte au XII Siècle*, by Gustave Schlumberger. His musical interest was reflected in copies of musical scores by Brahms, Beethoven and Mozart. His voracious curiosity was fed by extensive travel, which gave him a cosmopolitan, rather than a provincial view of the world around him.

Fathy's voluminous writings on city planning problems and his drawings and photographs of Nubian and Cycladic architecture are among the many manifestations of his multifacetted intellect. Rather than scattering his energies, however, he was able to bring them all to bear on his architecture, which he considered to be the mother of all the arts.

The third general principle of Fathy's work, and the one that most distinguished it from that of the Modern movement, was his belief in the need for appropriate technology in architecture. As explained by Ludwig Mies van der Rohe, one of the most famous apologists of Modernism, the primary goal of that philosophy was 'to express the technology of the times', because 'architecture is the will of an epoch translated into space'. This view encouraged a change in the architect's role from that of a master builder working to produce a socially and environmentally compatible building, to that of an individualist, striving to incorporate the latest technological advances into his or her work.

What Fathy shared with Mies van der Rohe, however, was an appreciation of the work of the German philosopher Immanuel Kant, but, characteristically, Fathy differed in his understanding of that philosophy. Where Mies reacted positively to Kant's conception of truth 'untouched by human experience' which led him to seek an abstract fitness of purpose for each small detail of his buildings, Fathy related more to what Kant called 'representations of imagination', which are totally subjective and therefore beyond rational proof. For Fathy, technology must be applied in a way appropriate to both its users and its context, and be controlled by what he once described as 'the innate knowledge that comes directly from the emotions without study or analysis, or from what psychology calls the subconscious'. He constantly appealed to all architects to temper scientific methods with a sensitivity for human needs. His approach to technology was closely related to the Greek meaning of the root of that word, *techne*, which stands for skill or craft, rather than the blind application of science. Through *techne* he felt that architecture could become a true arbiter between the highest achievements of human intelligence and the natural world, to the mutual benefit of both. Fathy believed that modern architecture failed to achieve Mies's mandate to 'express the technology of the times'. As he said at the University of Essex in a lecture entitled 'The Arab House in the Urban Setting' in 1970:

> The direction of every advance in technology has been towards the human mastery of the environment. However, until very recently human beings have always maintained a certain balance between his physical and spiritual being and the external world. Disruption of this balance may have a detrimental effect on us genetically, physiologically or psychologically and however fast technology advances, all change must be related to the rate of change in us as a species.[4]

The fourth principle that is consistent in Fathy's work is his belief in the idea of co-operative building, or what is now called 'self-help'. Having originally put this idea into practice in the construction of the village of New Gourna nearly fifty years ago, he was finally to see it accepted in principle throughout the world.

Opposite Traditional features were adopted by Fathy in his search for a new architectural language. He revitalized elements that were practical as well as decorative.

Above left A *malkaf* (wind catch) rises above a balcony with *mashrabiya* (wooden latticework screen) in medieval Cairo. Both allow cool air to circulate effectively.

Below left Roofline in medieval Cairo. Air flows in through the *malkaf*; warm air inside the house rises by convection and leaves through the *shukshaykha* (lantern dome).

Below right *Takhtabush*, a covered seating area between two courtyards. The difference in temperature between a hot paved courtyard and a cooler planted one creates a breeze by convection which flows through the dividing screen, cooling the seating area.

Above right Traditional Nubian mosque.

This page Fathy's buildings recast traditional forms.

Above left Fathy's mosque at New Gourna, 1947, emulates traditional Nubian forms (**opposite above right**). The height of the minaret is balanced with the mass of the dome towards the right.

Right Co-operative Centre, Kharga, 1970. The *maqa'ad* (loggia or outdoor 'room') takes advantage of shade and breeze from the courtyard.

Below left Sadat resthouse, Gharb Husayn 1981. Vaults and domes distinguished Fathy's buildings throughout his career. Traditional methods of circulating air often avoided the necessity for costly air-conditioning.

Fathy did not seek to theorize the profession, but saw the architect as working in partnership with people, and providing guidance on structural and aesthetic issues. He finally formalized this concept in his Institute for Appropriate Technology, through which he sought to expand on the ideas begun at New Gourna. When commissioned to assist in the design of the reconstruction of Sohar, in the Sultanate of Oman between 1970 and 1973, for example, where a fire had destroyed much of the commercial area of the city, he worked with local craftsmen to develop a lightweight roofing element using readily available, inexpensive materials, such as woven wire fabric and reeds, which he called a *baratsi* truss. This truss proved to be very light, structurally stable and weatherproof, and yet offered diverse architectural possibilities.

Fathy encouraged a deeper respect for the use of tradition in architecture, noting that the word itself comes from the Latin *tradere*, to carry forward or to transfer, and thus implies the cyclical renewal of life. He went further to identify this transfer with individual behaviour and its impact on society in general, by defining tradition as 'the social analogy of personal habit'. By doing so, he intimated that it is the responsibility of each architect to develop a heightened awareness of such habits, and to incorporate them sympathetically into each design. He also noted that tradition must be carried beyond the single career of an individual architect. Tradition represents the accumulated result of an ongoing evolution, and is loosely tied to the complicated cycles within each individual culture. He stressed that individual creativity need not be sacrificed by following tradition, because architecture is rooted in a continuity of experience established over a long period of time. For Fathy the rediscovery of traditional form also involved the search for a missing link in a cultural chain that had been cut by the intrusion of the industrial age, especially in his own country.

The sixth principle of Fathy's work is his determined attempt to reawaken a sense of cultural pride among his countrymen, and to make them aware of their rich architectural heritage. Because of his efforts, many young people are more informed about the Islamic architecture in the medieval part of Cairo, or they can be seen in the various research institutes through the city, studying the *Description de l'Egypte*, or Pauty, Weit and Prisse d'Avennes in their enthusiasm to see their city as it once was. This new awareness is no longer confined to Egypt alone, as Fathy's name has now become associated with the re-establishment of architectural tradition throughout the developing world.

In their rush towards what is euphemistically called progress, many developing countries have sought to eradicate the architecture of the past. One of Fathy's major contributions has been his effectiveness in warning others of the consequences. Throughout the Middle East in particular, his warnings have now led to a realization that a threat to an irreplaceable architectural heritage does exist, and major steps are now being taken to preserve and perpetuate that heritage.

Unrendered mud-brick arches at New Baris, Kharga Oasis, a community project curtailed by war in 1967.

1
Early Career: 1928–45

The earliest documented projects by Fathy, between 1928 and the Mansuriya Exhibition in 1937, demonstrate a remarkable evolution of ideas, which show his divergence from his classically based architectural training.

The Talka School of 1928, which is the first recorded project that Fathy completed after his graduation from architectural school, conforms to a classical Beaux-Arts education; only fragments of sketches remain, but these reveal the young architect's preference for classical details such as Doric columns, fretwork, dentils and acroterion. The Husni Omar Villa, the Sada al-Bariya Villa and the La Giardinara Kiosk, all completed in 1930, show the influence of trends predominating in Europe at this time. None of these bears any reference to the vernacular architecture of Egypt; rather, they incorporate modernist elements such as the use of concrete, steel and glass, and flat roofs. The Bosphore Casino and the *al-Sabah* journal building, completed in 1932, incorporate Art Deco chevron detailing reminiscent of Charles Rennie Mackintosh's remodelling of the Basset-Lowke House in Northampton, England, in 1916, which prefigured this fashion throughout Europe and the United States. These early projects by Fathy are significant because

Gouache of Abd al-Razik house (built 1941), exhibited at Mansuriya in 1937.
The picture observes the ancient Pharaonic convention of flattened perspectives.

they demonstrate his awareness of the trends in Europe, and the influence of their transmission to Egypt in books and journals.

From 1937 and 1938 the modernist language of Fathy's work began to be imbued with Arab vernacular details such as *mashrabiya* (wooden latticework screens), carved wooden balconies, arched doorways and windows and thick inclined walls. This blending of eastern and western styles continued in designs for the house for his brother Muhammad Fathy and for Mrs al-Harini (both 1938). Designs for public buildings, such as a hospital in Cairo in the same year, demonstrate a similar tendency.

While working on these commercial projects, Fathy was engaged in his own private research: attempting to identify the persistently occurring typologies of Islamic Cairo and developing his own repertoire of indigenous historical forms. Although never built, several designs for mud-brick residences that Fathy exhibited in Mansuriya in 1937 led to new preoccupations. These designs exist as a series of watercolour renderings of extraordinary beauty that have an idyllic and dreamlike quality. Although difficult to read at first in the standard architectural sense, because of the multiple perspective technique used in ancient Egyptian wall paintings, the gouaches have an astonishing graphic power. In the partially real, partially dreamlike world

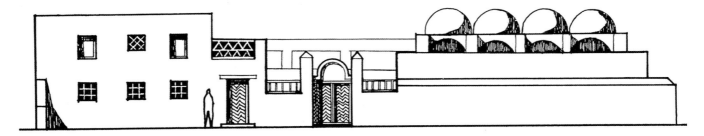

Elevation of the Royal Society of Agriculture project, Bahtim, 1941. Fathy's attempt to build the domes failed at first, leading him to search for new solutions to the challenge of inexpensive roofing.

Opposite Fatimid tombs from the late tenth century, south of Aswan.

that the paintings evoke, trees mythically become fire red or ice blue, and creatures of air, earth and water co-exist in a natural paradise in which the architecture itself seems almost selfconscious. There is a childlike innocence and compelling vision in these images reminiscent of the tapestries and weaving of the Ramsis Wissa Wassif atelier in Harraniya, which display the same unity with nature.

One of the first projects to be realized as a direct result of the Mansuriya Exhibition was a prototype farm for the Royal Society of Agriculture, built in Bahtim in 1941. This sizable self-contained complex proved to be a pivotal moment in the evolution of the architect's technique because it forced the issue of finding a method of building the vaults and domes shown in his watercolours. To be viable as a solution to the housing crisis in rural Egypt, that method had to eliminate costly building techniques.

The Bahtim complex consists of housing, a stable for cattle, granaries and a pigeon-cote, all organized within a boundary wall with one main gate. To provide a large open area for the cattle and to zone this area away from the living quarters, elements are once again strategically manipulated to provide specialized usage of open space. The granaries, which are of necessity very high for adequate natural ventilation as well as maximum storage capacity, become the dominant forms in the composition. The associations inspired by the idea of the granary, which was such an important building type

in ancient Egyptian history, were no doubt a very strong factor in their massing. Both the housing and the stables were designed with flat roofs to be framed with wood in the conventional way, which presented no technical problem, but the vaults and domes of the granaries were another matter. In trials for the construction, he attempted to build domes, vaults and walls from mud brick. His first attempts were unsuccessful – the domes collapsed – but the exploration that this initiated was the next important stepping stone in his career.

The collapse of the domes of the Royal Society of Agriculture Farm project was a disappointing shock for Fathy. At the suggestion of his brother Ali, he travelled south to Aswan to investigate Nubian mud-brick architecture, which has remained unchanged since the Pharaonic period. He also sought out several obscure examples of mud-brick arch construction from other periods and made expeditions to survey and photograph them.

Fathy's *Architecture for the Poor*, written nearly three decades after the fact, still conveys his sense of discovery and excitement at finding a structural system that would allow him to build with mud brick without the need for any supports. No issue is more basic to Fathy's work, or has caused more resistance to it, than his early choice of this material which has come to be so closely associated with his name.

While the religious monuments that were built in stone in ancient Egypt have survived, and are the part of its architectural heritage that usually attracts the most attention, the everyday life of the people themselves was acted out in mud-brick structures that were usually as ephemeral as the masons who built them. But the

EARLY CAREER: 1928–45

The structure of the Fatimid tombs was both practically robust and formally decorative, and helped to convince Fathy of the possibility of building in mud brick. The entrance arches show a characteristically Fatimid profile.

Below right Even where a building has begun to deteriorate, what remains of the dome demonstrates the structure's inherent strength.

vaulted areas behind the Temple of Ramses II near Aswan used by the priests to store grain offerings were built nearly 2000 years ago. Rarely seen by tourists, they are still standing.

Another example of durable mud-brick arch construction that Fathy saw were the Fatimid tombs on the main road leading south from Luxor. These reminders of Fatimid incursions into the last Nubian Christian strongholds in this area date back to 970, and began suffering more severe damage in the late 1960s due to lack of an annual plaster covering, but Fathy saw them while they were still relatively intact. The decorative finials and the gracefully curved individual domes of the mausoleums have a typically Fatimid line, with each distinctly different. The pioneering historian of Islamic art and architecture K. A. C. Creswell published surveys of each of them, stating that two exceptionally heavy rainy seasons had destroyed examples that had lasted for centuries.

A third example of mud-brick construction that Fathy saw near Aswan was the Deir al-Samaan (or St Simeon) monastery, some distance inland from Elephantine Island and the Nile, on the desert side. Then as now usually reachable only by camel or on foot, it is a stark desert outpost on a rock promontory overlooking the desert. Home to a community of monks obviously attracted by its isolation, it was built sometime in the late sixth century. The monastery uses large vault spans and showed Fathy how to add a second storey over a vaulted hall.

The fourth and least easily studied example of ancient mud-brick construction that Fathy saw was the Christian cemetery of Bagawat, deep in the desert with scores of large burial vaults and some houses still

standing. The arid desert climate has preserved them, with primitively but effectively formed squinches and domes configured in layers of now desiccated clay that convey practised skill and effective use of the material.

These case studies, combined with his knowledge of others, such as the Sassanian arch of Ctesiphon and the Uqaider desert palace near Karbala, Iraq, encouraged Fathy that mud brick was a logical and practical material from which to fabricate the new translation of indigenous architecture, a material as old as Egypt itself. This historical aspect, as well as the obvious analogic connection between the earth and the nation it represented, were strong factors behind his choice, equal to his desire to be free of a dependence on costly foreign materials such as concrete, steel and glass. The Second World War made these already scarce commodities even more difficult to obtain. More importantly, no matter what was available, they were still unaffordable for the average Egyptian *fellah* (peasant), while mud-brick construction is relatively cheap. All it requires is earth, straw, some cow dung, water and labour. No centring, scaffolding, supporting forms, reinforcing bars, cranes, rivets, bolts, welders or foreign concessions are required.

An ethnic rather than national designation, Nubia is a geographic region concentrated along the Nile, divided evenly by the border between Upper Egypt and the Sudan. The second cataract of the river at Wadi Halfa acts as a more natural dividing line between the Egyptian and Sudanese Nubians than the border itself.

The culture of the Nubians is very diverse. The only consistent link is the Nile itself, and yet the landscape around it constantly changes. In Upper Egypt, huge

Above Mason at work on the Greiss house, 1982, using traditional methods. Fathy combined the use of stone (seen in the background) with ancient mud-brick construction.

Left Ramesseum storage vaults, first century BC. Fathy was impressed by the durability of the self-supporting mud-brick arches. After almost 2000 years the masons' finger marks are still visible in many of the bricks.

Fathy travelled extensively to study historical precedents for traditional building.

Above The Christian cemetery at Bagawat.

Opposite, above and below left The Ramesseum.

Opposite, below right The monastery of St Simeon, or Deir al-Samaan.
It was here that Fathy noticed the use of a secondary arch which allowed
a flat floor to be constructed above the main arch.

Contemporary vernacular tomb at Abu al-Riche. The dome indicates the high religious status of the occupant. Structures of this kind are still commonly found in Upper Egypt.

sand dunes come almost to the edge of the river bank, but towards the Wadi Halfa the banks flatten out into wider areas strewn with large boulders, and acacia groves begin to soften the plains beyond. The Kanuzi Nubians, faced with the challenge of a harsh, treeless environment, and the problem of roofing over spaces without wood for beams or supporting members for centring, have perpetuated a building technique that has been used in Egypt since at least the thirteenth century BC, as in the Ramesseum, the mortuary complex of Ramses II. Located across the Nile from Luxor, this was the utilitarian storehouse part of the Temple, holding the provisions for the Pharaohs' afterlife. The mud bricks used in the construction of the granaries still bear the finger marks of the masons who built them.

The technique used by the Kanuzi was published at the beginning of this century by several noted scholars, but was brought to public attention most dramatically by Fathy, who proposed it as an inexpensive solution to the critical housing shortage facing the Egyptian peasant. In brief, this method of construction shows a great intuitive understanding of the laws of statics and resistance of materials by utilizing the compressive strength of mud brick, while avoiding tensile or bending stresses, which it cannot resist. The vaults that form the basis of the system are made in a parabolic shape that will keep the material in compression only.

Typically, the vaults begin with the erection of a kick-wall built up against the end wall to the desired height of the space to be constructed. The masons, usually working in pairs, make a free-form outline of the parabolic vault in mud on the end wall as a guide. The proper shape of the curve is crucial for structural success, and learning how to lay it out without surveying tools of any kind requires long hours of practice, with skills often passed from father to son.

After this mud guide-line has partially dried the masons trim the rough edges with a sharp adze before applying the first course of mud bricks to it. The bricks used for the vault have a higher proportion of straw to mud, which makes them much lighter than those used for the walls, and each brick is scored with two finger grooves while still wet in order to give better adherence to the mud mortar.

A starter brick is laid straight up at the base of the vault line on both sides, and mud mortar is packed on it to form a wedge that is thinner at the top of the bricks and wider at the bottom. This sets the angle for each of the vault courses to follow, so that they incline toward the end wall in compression rather than remaining perpendicular to the ground, which would make them collapse. As each course of bricks is added, the masons stagger the joint lines between each row of bricks to assist bending and gradually continue to make the mortar thicker at the base of the arch than at the peak so that the entire assembly leans on the end wall.

This purposeful inclining of the vault as it is put into place accounts for the characteristically massive vertical end wall and sloped front edge of the vaults that are usually found in these mud brick buildings. The recommended span for vaults built this way is 3 metres, and 5 metres is the maximum diameter for domes using vaults as buttressing, which limits the width of the spaces that can be built using this method. Aside from the favourable aesthetic considerations, the vault also has the advantage of allowing more natural air ventilation in the higher space that it creates. If the

Contemporary vernacular house at Abu al-Riche, showing the vault construction Fathy appropriated in the 1940s. After the erection of the end wall and side walls, the vault is built in inclined layers, each course leaning on the last against the end wall; the building is finally closed with a wall at the front.

Gouache of a utopian landscape. The type of buildings Fathy has drawn here show his wider intentions. Revitalizing traditional building techniques was as important for Egyptian architecture as it was for promoting a renewed sense of national identity after colonial rule.

ends of the vault are provided with open grilles, a convection cycle can be created that is difficult to achieve in the flat-roofed, wood-beamed houses further up the Nile.

The use of dome forms has been restricted by the Nubians to buildings with religious functions, such as mosques and the tombs of holy men. There are exceptions, however, where more conical shapes are used over purely utilitarian structures, but care is taken in these instances to avoid a hemispherical outline.

The religious connotations of the dome form may come from its symbolic connection with the sky vault, as indicated by the Arabic word *qubba* for dome from the Aramaic *qubtha*, the vault of heaven. The use of the dome for tombs in particular has been ascribed to the Shi'ite influence of the Fatimids who entered Egypt from North Africa in 969 to found Cairo.

Nubian house forms were also affected by the conversion to Islam, mainly in ways related to privacy and the separation of the sexes. Archaeological excavations near the Wadi Halfa have shown that the houses of the Christian era consisted of a string of rooms grouped around a single entry space with no central open area being used. The courtyard, as a device for protecting private family areas from the view of guests, eventually appeared as a standard feature in the houses of all the Nubian groups although both the size and the function of the rooms surrounding it vary greatly from Egypt to the Sudan. In the village of Abu al-Riche, near Aswan, for example, two rooms that are always a common denominator are the *mandara* and the *khayma*. The *mandara*, which is set aside for guests, is usually located close to the main entrance and placed in such a way that the view into the interior of the house is blocked. All windows from the room face the street only, and it is normally vaulted and spacious compared to the other spaces of the house, indicating the importance of hospitality in this society. The *khayma* is a flat-roofed loggia, covered over with palm leaves for coolness, that is located on the private side of the courtyard and used as a sitting and sleeping area for the family, especially during the summer when the temperature in Upper Egypt can reach 55 degrees centigrade.

In the Wadi Halfa region there may be rooms given over to guests, where a *diwan*, or sitting room, is reserved for wedding receptions only, a *diwan hasil* is used as a social space for women, and the *mandara*, which serves the same function as in Aswan, is provided with an additional antechamber, or *dahliz*, to insulate it even further from the private family areas.

In addition to the innovative construction methods and spatial forms and organizations used by the Nubians, their method of exterior decoration in painted scribed earth is unique, and shows a high level of empathy for the plastic and artistic potential of the material, using mud plaster as a protective as well as a decorative medium.

The construction of the Aswan High Dam, which began in 1960, led to the flooding of the majority of the Nubian homeland, obliterating most of the traditional villages where this style of architecture existed. Prior to the flooding, the Egyptian Minister of Culture, in an enlightened gesture acknowledging the the rare beauty of the work, invited a group of architects, artists, photographers, writers, poets, and musicians to visit this area, to record what they saw before its destruction. Fathy was part of the group, and was greatly moved by this farewell visit to the heartland of a people whose architecture had so greatly influenced his own, both technically and intellectually. As a result of the trip, he produced an extensive survey of the buildings he saw.

Fathy related the story of travelling in a car one day and noticing a colt running freely along the side of the road, then slowing down and returning to its mother to feed. 'The Nubians', he said,

> have done the same thing. Although there a million options…to choose from … they showed a preference for the group model, just as the colt went back to its mother. All the buildings [we saw] were shouting: Be free … dream as much as you like. This freedom, combined with Science and Technology, are all that is needed to make the Arabian horse a true champion. The Nubian village [is] an example of balance between dream and reality in expression and freedom is linked to a point of reference … [it] does not mean searching for the new.[1]

With this system in hand, Fathy was finally prepared to combine it with his conviction about the appropriateness of mud brick as the proper material for a truly indigenous Egyptian architecture and what may be termed a 'thesis of space', pieced together in medieval Cairo to create a highly individual architecture.

The Kallini residence, which is the first trial design of this combination, shows the same tendencies toward ambitious scale in the formal reception spaces, especially in its dominant central *qa'a*. The raised

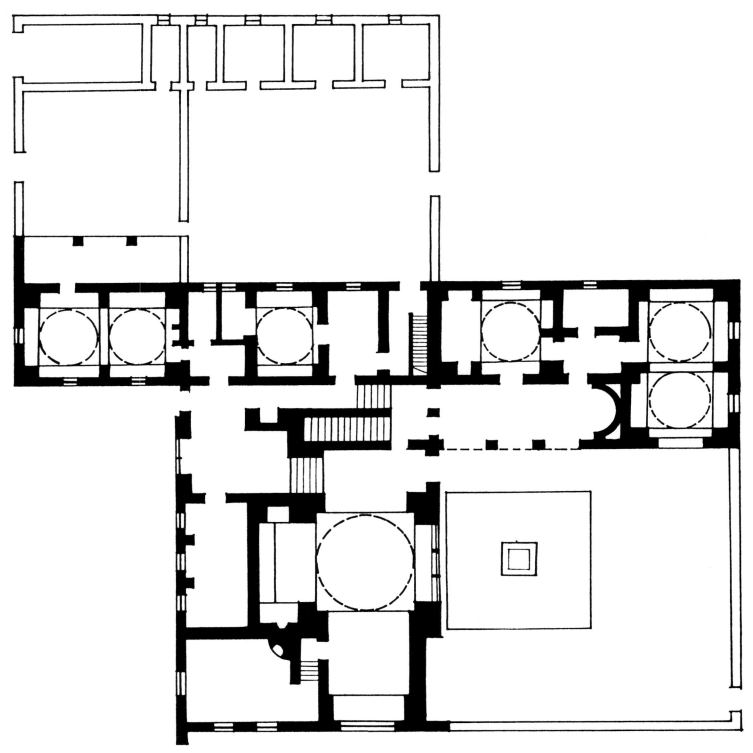

Plan for the Kallini house (1945), one of Fathy's most ingenious designs.
The clear differentiation between public and private spaces is maintained while
allowing easy access to a shared courtyard (at the bottom right-hand corner),
with an arcade serving as an intermediate zone.

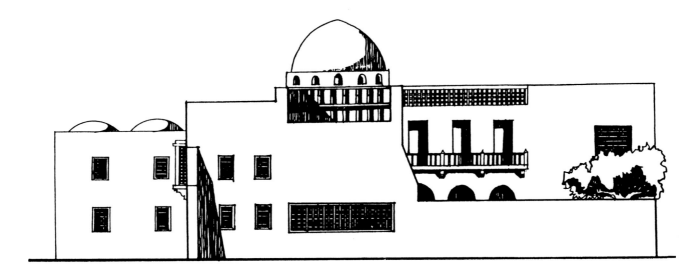

platform for guests commands a view through a North African-style *maghribi* (horseshoe arch) which looks out over a large court. Its shape and proportion emphasize this powerful symbol of the Arab Classical period. Other details evoke this tradition, such as carefully crafted wooden railings angled to join the balcony to the springing line of the arch, emphasizing the interior focus of the building; and windows reminiscent of those found to the north, particularly in the domestic architecture of the Mamluk period in Lebanon. While Fathy may have been aware of such variations within that extremely rich architectural period, thanks to the historical research he undertook in other countries, it cannot be said with absolute certainty that this particular detail was inspired by the countless windows of this type in that area. The combination of forms that he uses, however, does show how Fathy was able to draw upon a wide range of sources, and here he skilfully evokes two of the most significant periods of the Muslim past.

The direction of the prevailing breeze here did not encourage the use of a *malkaf* (wind catch) placed in direct sequence with the formal public courtyard. Local conditions dictated that the *malkaf* should be located directly above the main *iwan*, bringing cool air to honoured guests. Such a position is rare among the many designs in which the architect uses a wind catch,

as direct sequencing between the major courtyard, *malkaf* and *qa'a* seems to become a predictable constant in nearly all of the longitudinal sections of that work that follows. The result of that design is a long, high wall opposite the smaller *iwan*, incorporating an impressively high, two-storey window, covered with a large *mashrabiya* (wooden latticework screen) overlooking the open courtyard. In scale, this window recalls one in the Manzil al-Sinnari which Fathy greatly admired, and another at the Bayt al-Suhaymi, both fine examples of medieval houses in Cairo.

In spite of its having been done very early in the architect's career, the Kallini house is one of the most ingeniously organized of all of Fathy's projects. The cross-axial positioning of both the formal and informal courtyards allows them to relate directly to the segments of the house to which they correspond, and yet to be physically and visually separated from each other. It is this ingenious basic design concept itself, rather than any simple expedients, which achieves privacy. By choosing this dynamic, spiralling, cross-axial device, Fathy was able to use an enfilade of rooms running through the centre of the plan to achieve an unselfconscious and more comfortable division of two separate worlds.

One of the most important concerns of this entire design effort was the retention of the self-contained quality of the courtyard, which had slowly evolved over time as a peaceful respite from the outside world. One of the Arabic names for house, in fact, is *sakan*, related to peace and purity, and *sakina* is a word that Fathy often used to try to describe the elusive quality he sought in the courtyards that he designed, which he described as follows:

> The word *sakina* means peaceful and holy, while the word *harim* which means woman and is related to the work *haram*, meaning sacred, denote the family living quarters within. This peace and holiness, this feminine inwardness, this atmosphere of a house for which 'domesticity' is so inadequate a description, is so fragile that the least little rupture in the frail walls that guard it allow it to escape.[2]

Of all of the projects that he designed, the Kallini house presents one of the best examples of *sakina* that Fathy ever achieved, and remains as a clear expression of his deep concern for establishing a place of refuge within the home that could not be touched by the world outside the walls that he created.

The Hamdi Seif al-Nasr house, on the bank of Birkit Fayyum, is a highly compromised version of the original design, as indicated in one of Fathy's most eloquent gouaches (pp. 42–43). The result of several redesigns commissioned by a wealthy landowner, it was intended to be used only on periodic visits to the property.

Fathy's first design was an ambitiously fortress-like structure planned on a very similar scale to the Kallini house (pp. 40–41).

Manzil al-Sinnari, Cairo. This shows one of the largest surviving medieval balconies with *mashrabiya* (wooden latticework screen). Not only is the structure functional – it diffuses glare, allows privacy for those looking out and provides effective ventilation – its fine decorative construction also shows masterful craftsmanship.

Opposite Elevation of the Kallini house, showing the *malkaf* (wind catch) directly below the central dome. Sloped pilasters (such as the one projecting from the wall of the main part of the building) add strength to supporting walls and present a dramatic profile.

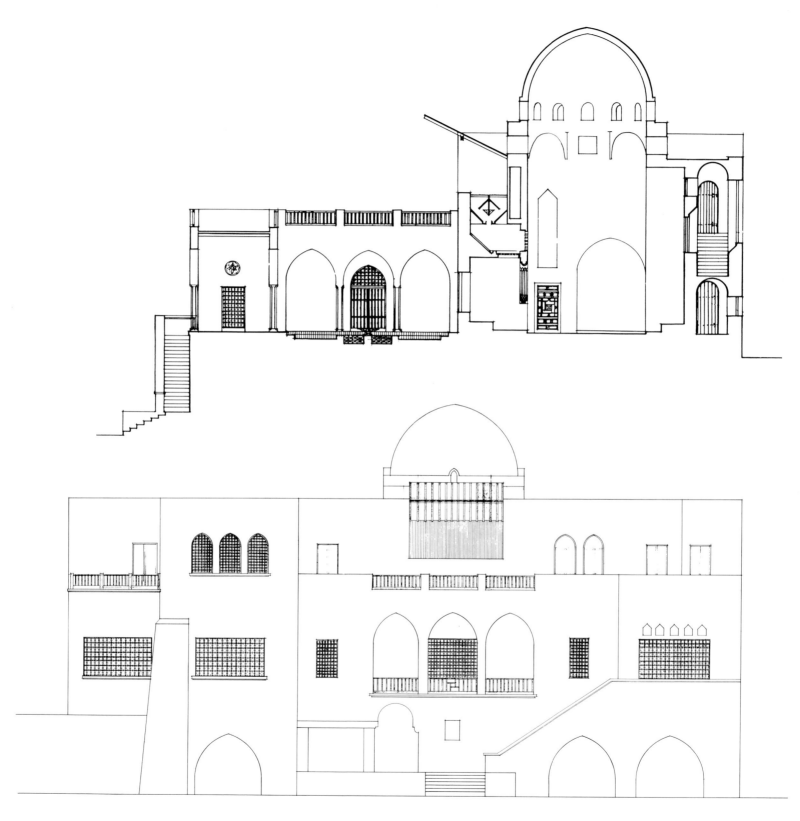

Below Preliminary plan of the Hamdi Seif al-Nasr house (1942).

Opposite Section (**above**) and elevation (**below**) of the Hamdi Seif al-Nasr house, preliminary design. Note the *malkaf* (wind catch) on the left of the dome, directing a current of air past a *salsabil* (cooling plate) wetted by a constant trickle from the earthenware *zir* (water pot) suspended above it, providing humidity.

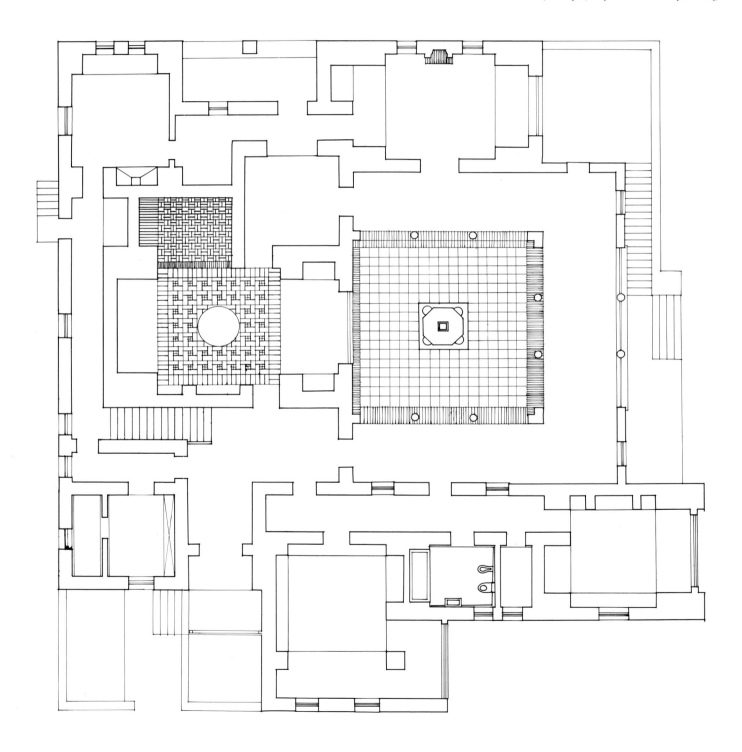

Gouache of the Hamdi Seif al-Nasr house. Fathy's watercolours demonstrate buildings in close harmony with their natural surroundings; here the blossoming trees complement the natural earth colours of the building itself.

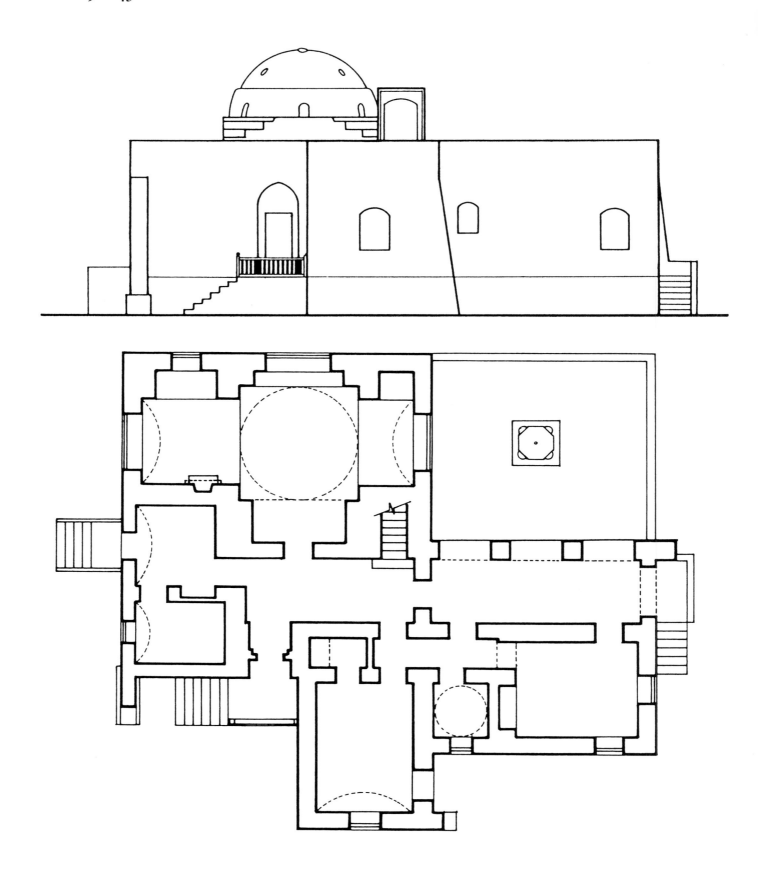

Survey plan and elevation of the Hamdi Seif al-Nasr house. Reduced in scale from the preliminary plans, the final building shows a more economical use of space and incorporates an open courtyard, here also used as an entry.

The plan is organized around a large square interior courtyard, with public reception and dining spaces falling to one side of the axis through the courtyard, and private family spaces on the other. The *qa'a*, with its attached *malkaf* oriented to bring in the cool air from the central court, mediates between the public and private zones, to be available to both. The architect's gouache for this proposal is one of his most exquisite, expressing total unity between earth, building and sky.

The reorganized and scaled down version of the resthouse that was finally built in 1945 occupies the tip of a narrow peninsula projecting into Lake Fayyum, with a long driveway leading up to it. Surrounded by a mirror of water glistening at midday through the mature trees that line the drive, the entire scene suggests a dream-like quality as one approaches.

The *qa'a* has a direct visual relationship with a formal, walled exterior courtyard. The large *malkaf* was altered for use as a stair to the roof (p. 46). This alteration prevents a measured evaluation of a contemporary usage of a *malkaf*, in one of the few installations of a design by Fathy.

The courtyard has been altered from its central interior location in the early scheme to the exterior of the house, most probably because the site enjoys a high degree of privacy and a spectacular view. It is raised upon a high plinth which he accentuates by leaving the rusticated band of mud bricks on the base rather than plastered smooth as they are on the upper part of the house. This plinth is intended to prevent periodic flooding and to provide a raised platform from which to take advantage of the magnificent views from three sides of the building.

The formal courtyard, as the key element of the composition, is located so that anyone entering the house is guided up to it by stairs, taken along a wide shaded arcade on its side and given framed views across it to the tree-lined approach to the house. It also acts as the final link in the entry sequence by providing foreground scale for the water that is presented after turning into the *qa'a*. Rather than just being used as a patio for outdoor sitting, the courtyard is thus cleverly used as an ordering device, to do double duty in the formal circulation sequence by first visually orienting the visitor back to the point of entry, and then acting as a pivot to present the full impact of the view to the water from the most impressive space in the building. On the private or 'support' side of the house both the master bedroom and the guest bedroom have direct, uninterrupted views to the lake.

Fathy chose to use timber framing in this house, except for the mud-brick dome which covers the *qa'a*. This seems curious at first, considering that by then he had the ability to use vaults and domes throughout. It seems likely that his intention was to go to the extra expense of a timber frame in order to take advantage of the flat roof as a traditional outdoor sleeping area. It is plausible that he was still mentally working through the images and concepts begun in the Kallini house nearly eight years before, and that this was supported by the fact that timber was readily available on site. A dominant horizontal expression of the roof line relates the house to both the flatness of the land and the water around it. In addition, the consistent horizontality of the roof line accentuates the scale and importance of the *qa'a*, giving it an impressiveness befitting the economic stature of a wealthy landowner.

Hamdi Seif al-Nasr house. What was originally intended as a *malkaf* or wind catch (**top**) was altered by the owner for use as a staircase (**below**). This is the last example of Fathy's overt use of a *malkaf* on a domestic scale.

Opposite Stepped squinches support the dome, resolving its round base with the squarely set walls. The *umriyad* (piercing the top of the dome) and the other windows provide light within.

At about this time, Fathy was working on a resthouse for the Chilean Nitrate Company at Safaga on the Red Sea, almost midway between Cairo and Luxor. The plan and elevation of this project reflect a highly ordered series of spaces which clearly indicate the status of those using them. There is a clear distinction made between the repetitive spaces for the workers, each with a kitchen, bath and sitting area, and the end unit intended for use by more senior staff. This repetition, in combination with the exaggerated vertical scale seen in the Kallini and Hamdi Seif al-Nasr houses, provides a sense of grandeur in what would otherwise have been a purely utilitarian expression. The architect reinforces it in door and window openings, an upper level arcade, and in side-wall buttressing. The section also indicates an extension of this repetition through to every element of the structure.

Not all of Fathy's efforts at this time were blessed with the same degree of success that he achieved at Safaga, Bahtim and the Said and al-Nasr houses. He also experienced his first taste of the special kind of resistance he was to face in Egypt for the rest of his career. The basic issues involved economics and architectural style.

At the outset, the opportunity to build twenty new houses to replace those lost in a flash flood for the community of Izbit al-Basri, near Cairo, seemed like an excellent chance to demonstrate the versatility and economy of Fathy's rediscovered construction techniques. After protracted discussions with the local Red Crescent Society that was co-ordinating and sponsoring the rebuilding effort, Fathy persuaded them to allow him to build one prototype demonstration unit. This test house, which took only forty days to build, was very spacious, with two large bedrooms, a kitchen-dining room, and a bath and storage room forming an 'L' around an enclosed, private courtyard. Even on the restrictive budget which Fathy set himself in order to dramatize the practicality of his methods, he was able to incorporate many of the spatial ideas and details that had begun to evolve in his other designs.

The *qa'a* ensemble of *durqa'a* and *iwan*, which has been used as a formal reception area in more affluent circumstances, is here scaled down and adapted for use as a sleeping area, with the *iwan* becoming a sleeping alcove. Other ideas, such as the indirect entry, claustra-work serving both as a ventilator at the end of the vault and as wall decoration, and even features such as

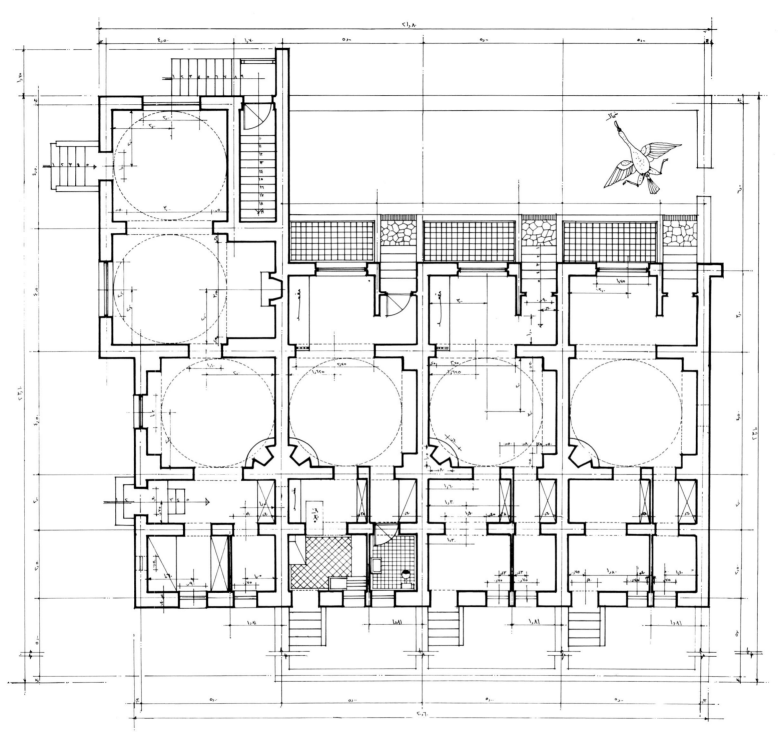

House for the Chilean Nitrate Company, Safaga (1942). The plan shows sophisticated planning of interior space.

Opposite Three apartments are joined by a common balcony overlooking the Red Sea. A fourth apartment, probably for more senior staff, is on the right.

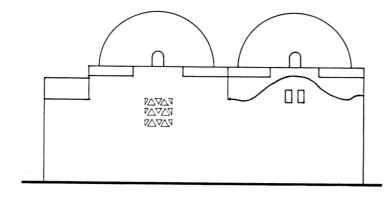

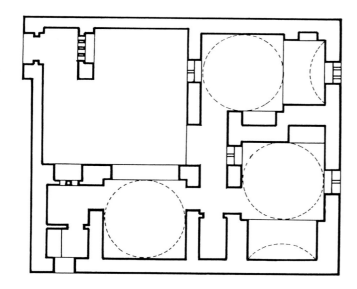

Elevation and plan, Izbit al-Basri. This prototype for cheap and functional housing was commissioned by the Red Crescent Society. It was built, but was rejected (and demolished) in favour of more expensive concrete blocks erected by a competitive contractor, who was paid a percentage of the final cost. This sort of problem was to become very familiar.

coloured glass *umriyad* stars inserted in the scaled-down domes, were able to be included, giving the villagers of Izbit al-Basri spatial experiences similar to those once enjoyed by the wealthiest merchants of Cairo.

It was then that he first began to understand the diabolical workings of what he was later to call the 'contractor system', a catchphrase used as a scathing denunciation of a tacit, ingrained arrangement that rewards architects, contractors and suppliers with a percentage of the total construction cost, thereby discouraging any incentive at all for savings. Fathy's test house was pulled down, and the contract was awarded to a scheme which proposed flat-roofed concrete units for a considerably higher cost.

Another gouache, frequently listed as being of the Abd al-Razik house (p. 22), is one of the most lyrical of the entire group that Fathy did, along with that of the Hamdi Seif al-Nasr house, which is chronologically close to it. There were, in fact, two separate houses done for the Abd al-Razik family. The first was for Isma'il Abd al-Razik for his estate near Abu Girg, in Upper Egypt in 1941, and the second for Hassan Abd al-Razik in Bani Mazar, which was commissioned two years later. The gouache is for the first of these, and it represents a pivotal point in the architect's philosophical development, as is evident in the recorded progress of the design. This record, which consists of fragmentary studies on fragile yellow tracing paper, shows how the design becomes incrementally more refined in three succeeding stages. The first of these stages shows two separate zones, with the formal reception on one side, and the large private family area grouped around a spacious rectilinear inner courtyard on the other, accessible through a double gate. In order to segregate guests from the family, the entrance to the guest area is put on the side of the house directly opposite the double gate, through a long, narrow pergola that runs along a wall dividing the two sections. This linear, processional entry continues inside, with an extended corridor taking visitors and guests into a rectilinear reception room, which is placed to one side of the entry. The entry door to this reception room, which is set up on a perpendicular cross-axis with the corridor, lines up directly with a large, projecting *mashrabiya* screen on its opposite wall, which in turn opens onto a small, square enclosed courtyard beyond.

The second scheme retains the separation of family and guest entrances on different sides of the house. The family enters through what would normally be considered a back door, after crossing a large courtyard. A long, east–west corridor replaces the north–south wall of the first plan as the device that the architect uses to segregate public and private functions, and a lush and elaborate garden with an apsidal end wall is cleverly arranged to provide a view for both areas.

The third and final version of the house, to which the gouache relates, is more compact than the two preceding designs, returning to the use of a north–south wall as a divider as in the first version. The formal reception functions are located to the left of the main public entry, and project forward into a garden of their own, as if to welcome those walking across it. A tall, elegantly formed *qa'a* is the major architectural element of this segment, with a high-stepped parapet around it that is rarely seen elsewhere in the architect's work. This stately *qa'a* is actually the last of a series of rooms running from the front of the house to the back, with a lower counterpart. This lower room, presumably

intended as an antechamber, has a *mashrabiya* screen positioned to allow a good view of the paved court beyond, and a stepped claustra-work parapet on its dropped roof that creates a subtle layering effect with the crest of the *qa'a* behind it. The entry to the reception area itself, which is shown projecting out to the left toward the far edge of the area paved in blue tile, leads into a large vestibule, which opens into a long corridor running at a cross-axis to it, in an arrangement that is very similar to the first scheme. This corridor, which is nearly two metres wide and eleven metres long, and has a very thick wall on its right-hand side that extends to become the garden wall seen in the elevation, spans the entire width of the house between the lower antechamber in the foreground, and the *qa'a* at the rear of the house.

As is common in Fathy's work, the entry door is deeply recessed into the wall itself, with a high, arched reveal over it which gives a sense of the massiveness of the mud-brick construction. This recess creates cool, deep shadow lines on the inner face of the door jamb, and adds a feeling of mystery and serenity to the elevation. The family quarters assume pride of place on the right-hand side of the central wall. The small gate, walkway and offset entrance were secondary, with the more frequently used entry being located at the back, through a redesigned pergola that extends perpendicular to the house along the same north–south axis that is used for the central dividing wall. This long entrance walkway is bracketed by a high wall that protects it from outside view on one side, and opens up to an inner courtyard and servants quarters, partially screened by an arcade, on the other. The family walkway ends in a two-car garage, which is placed far

Two studies in gouache for the al-Razik villa.

Above This study shows a balcony with *mashrabiya* projecting from the main section. The flattened perspective is characteristic of Pharaonic paintings.

Right The upper storey shades the courtyard, a feature common to both studies, while the elevation shows significant change from the original.

enough away from the house so as to not intrude upon it, and yet is within easy walking distance. In spite of its secondary role, the front door to the private part of the house is elegantly detailed, with a series of brackets over it that also emphasize the depth of the wall in a more delicate way, and masterfully punctuate a visual progression along the cross-axis. These brackets also appear in a country house for Mrs Raymond Eid for her farm called 'Sharkieh' near Zagazig, designed in 1948. His sketches show Fathy's fondness for recycling pleasing details in a new way. These brackets are a stylized version of *muqarnas* (suspended vaults), greatly simplified here for construction in mud brick, and are combined with a stair that approaches the doorway indirectly from the right, in the manner of the entrance to the *maqa'ad* (raised loggia) of the Bayt al-Suhaymi in Cairo. There is a north-facing, double-arched *maqa'ad* here as well, on the ground floor next to the stair.

Although this *maqa'ad* is shown opening up into a blind arcade in the gouache, Fathy's plan for the house shows it as being accessible from openings behind each vault with perhaps only one of these openings intended to be used as a doorway, and the other as a *mashrabiya* screen. Directly behind this lower portion of the facade, of which the *maqa'ad* is a very prominent part, lies the living area, with a fireplace in one corner, and a low bench running its entire length along one wall. The chimney for this fireplace, which would normally protrude at the far left-hand side of the *maqa'ad* segment, is not shown in the elevation, hinting at the architect's desire to allow the higher, cross-axial segment to predominate, which is also indicated by the outwardly stepping parapet that visually brackets each end of it.

Fathy's representational technique provides an intentional link to Pharaonic wall paintings, which allowed the artist to portray multiple views of figures and landscapes simultaneously, subtly evoked in order to establish a subconscious link with the past in the mind of the viewer and to give his architecture a timeless aspect. As in Fathy's memorable gouache of the Hamdi Seif al-Nasr house, the trees that are shown in the Isma'il Abd al-Razik watercolour are particularly noteworthy, as he seems to look deep inside them and portray the hidden life-force within. Where the cherry tree of the Nasr house is fire red, the citrus trees here are pale blue, in a spectral translation of the sense of coolness that they provide in such a hot, arid region.

The Hamed Said house, which Fathy began in 1942, has in retrospect proved to be one of the most critical pieces in the puzzle of his professional development. Said was both encouraging and critical, open-minded and yet involved in the design process. Both men moved in the same circle in Cairo, and both were concerned with national identity in relation to a colonial presence.

Said and his wife, who are both artists, had had a studio which they called 'Tangezia' in the Muqataam hills, about an hour's walk from the Citadel in Cairo, and when highway construction forced the demolition of their house, they sought another, more permanent residence where they could both live and work in peace. In trying to recapture the monastic spirit of 'Tangezia', they set out in search of a suitably isolated spot in what was then mostly countryside close to Cairo, finally finding an ideal site near the village of Marg in 1942. Photographs of this area taken at that time show a verdant paradise of thickly clustered doum-palm trees and papyrus that enchanted them. Fathy often stayed with them in a tent that they had put up on their land, to get a better feeling for its character before the design process began.

Attempting to utilize what Said has called 'the simplest means to achieve the highest ends', the architect and his clients aimed at a modest but clear architectural expression of their joint belief in building in harmony with nature. The result was a simple structure made up of an enclosed, domed, studio space with an adjoining *iwan* for sleeping and a vaulted loggia that was completely open on one side to create the architectural equivalent of the tent from which they had come to relate so completely to the land. Said, who refers to Fathy as a *muallim benna* or master builder, calls his mud-brick architecture 'pottery and building at the same time'. As Fathy himself has described the use of earth in construction, it is an ideal material in that it is

> modelled by the craftsman, by the artisans, and man [is] putting something of himself into the material and radiating something into it, giving it something that [is] re-radiated back to man, along with the essence of the material, and doing him good. The principle of accretion allows for the constant interaction of man and material and environment.[3]

That harmony was so evident in the simple and closely interrelated open and closed components that Fathy produced at Marg that Said asked for an addition to it, which was built three years later, in 1945.

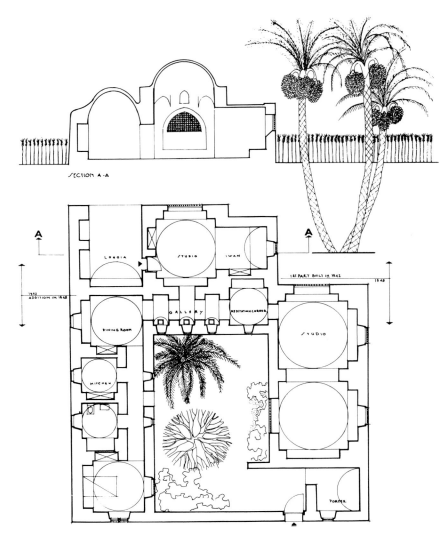

Elevation and plan of the Hamed Said house (1942–45). The upper section of the plan shows what was built in 1942; it was later extended – as shown in the lower section of the plan – to incorporate a larger courtyard and more living space. The drawing demonstrates a remarkably seamless integration of the two phases.

The only example of a large vaulted entrance by Fathy, visible at the left of the picture. The space was originally intended as a semi-outdoor studio for the owner, a painter.

Opposite, above Fathy (right) with Hamed Said.

Below left Hamed Said house, showing a corner of the internal courtyard, with an ancient Pharaonic plaque incorporated into the wall at the centre of the picture.

Below right The subsidiary vaults over a gallery show a rustic mud-plaster finish.

Carefully avoiding the trees near the existing studio, Fathy wrapped the new part of the house around them, creating an inner courtyard that served to join the first and second parts together.

In this addition, a gallery running the entire length of the original enclosed studio and *iwan* makes the transition between it and a second enlarged studio on one side of the court. The more utilitarian spaces used for cooking, dining and sleeping are grouped on the other. This gallery terminates in a so-called 'meditation corner' that is strategically placed to take advantage of the best view of the inner court and alternately widens

and narrows according to the positioning of the structural pilasters that the architect uses to support the skylight roof above it. Windows are placed in the narrow spaces between the pilasters, to allow framed slices of the court to be seen through them. In complete fulfilment of the clients' wishes, the spatial effects that Fathy has created, especially in this gallery space, far surpass the simple means used to achieve it, and to redirect a phrase that Said has used to describe the Pharaonic busts that he has displayed in this gallery: 'The organic presence, pulse and mystery are all there.' Far more than just a corridor joining one part of the house to another, this gallery has an almost cloister-like feeling, and becomes another of the architect's signature spaces, appearing whenever similar kinds of bilateral programmatic requirements call for more than a purely utilitarian solution, such as at the Stopplaere house that was to follow soon afterwards.

In its final form the house seems almost seamless in its planning, making it difficult to believe that it was built in two separate phases. Once completed, it soon began to serve as the meeting place for a group that calls itself 'the Friends of Art and Life'. This group, which feels that the purpose of all artistic endeavour is to form a connection between people and the environment, also believes that architecture, more than any other art, must be conditioned by it. Fathy's house, then, is a nearly perfect expression of the principles of this group, and has become an ideal venue for the weekly meetings that still take place there. These meetings, which were once held in the central courtyard and frequently included Fathy as well as other intellectuals from various branches of the arts, are now being held against the backdrop of the single wall that closes off the court, and provides a secondary entrance into it. These meetings usually include invited guests with many diverse interests and frequently begin with an extended opening statement by Said, followed by discussion and possibly a special showing of the work of one of the guests or members of the group, which is typically set up inside the house itself. These exhibitions may include sculpture, painting, fabric, pottery or jewelry.

Said has characterized many of the artists today as 'fractional' in that they do not respond or contribute directly to the culture in which they work. In the past, the function of the artist was to express a unified reality in a way that did not break with the traditions or conventions of society. Rather than being judged on the basis of compartmentalized individuality or a shocking anti-social statement, creative effort was gauged by the success of a specific work of art or architecture in promoting a renewed insight into the value of life. Parallels between his views and those of Hassan Fathy are obvious, and recall a time when the intellectual vitality of these two men, as well as that of Ramsis Wissa Wassif, founder of Harraniya Craft Centre, were in full force. Wissa Wassif, who taught with Fathy at the School of Fine Arts in Cairo, was, like Hamed Said, greatly influenced by the teachings of Habib Gorgy, who stressed the high level of creativity in the past and its innate presence in the national character. In 1941, Wissa Wassif, who had been trained as an architect in France and had served an apprenticeship with the well known sculptor Muhammad Mukhtar, began a creative experiment in Cairo to test Gorgy's theories. Using weaving as the medium, he selected children from a nearby village to be the artists, in the belief that they would manifest the innate creativity that Gorgy spoke of. That experiment has finally led to the establishment of the Ramsis Wissa Wassif Art Centre in Harraniya near Cairo, where the tangible proof of this belief can be clearly seen. Fathy was closely connected with the establishment of the village and the principles used there had a profound influence on his own work. Along with Ramsis Wissa Wassif, Fathy and Said formed an intellectual triumvirate sharing similar beliefs about the need to re-establish a distinct Egyptian personality that would supersede what they perceived to be the rapidly growing western influence in their country.

The ugly, uncontrolled urban sprawl of Cairo has now moved out to Marg, and the special vision of the future that Said, his wife and Fathy saw there has not been enough to exempt it from the same fate that has overtaken the rest of the lush green countryside that once surrounded the city. The couple have now been forced to build a low wall across the front of the outdoor vaulted room that once served as their viewing platform to the natural world they loved so much, and they have turned inward toward the past. In spite of this onslaught of concrete and steel, the owners remain where they are and the meetings go on, seeming now to be more of a memorial service than a voice for the future. The house, symbol of everything they believe in, remains at the centre of that memory.

Studio of the Hamed Said house, built onto the original building in 1945. The studio also accommodates furniture designed by Fathy.

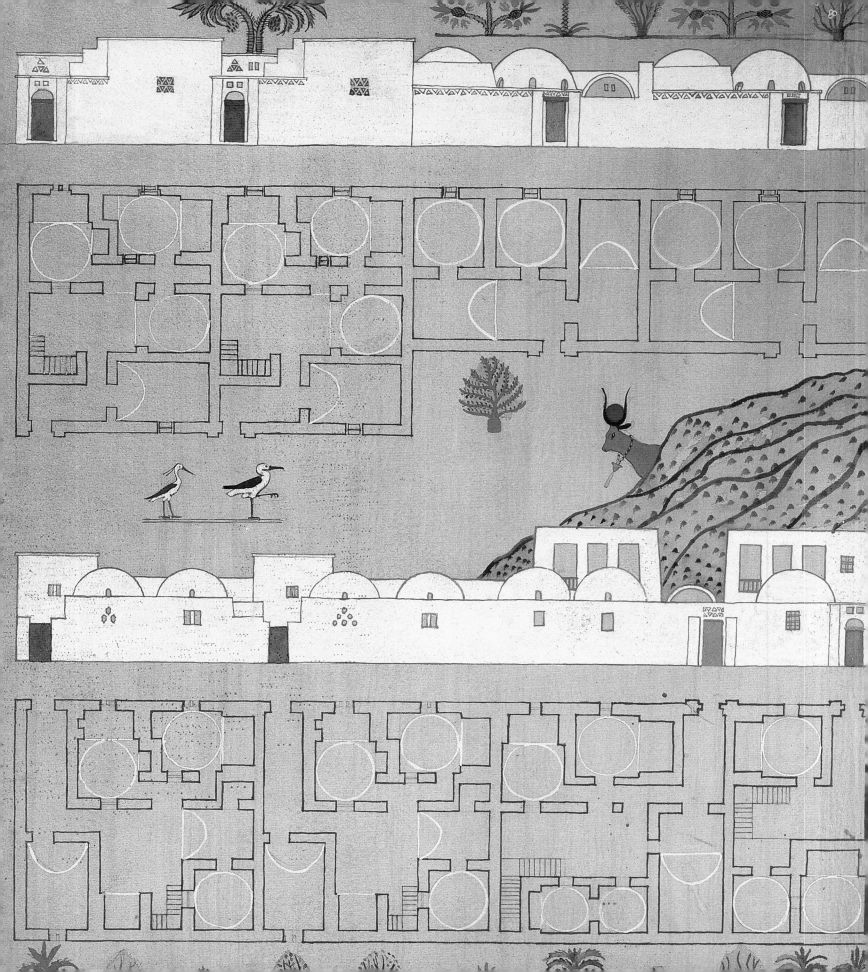

2
New Gourna: 1945–47

Fathy's early successes in the use of mud brick as a building material in Bahtim brought him to the attention of the Egyptian Department of Antiquities, who were looking for an inexpensive way to relocate the village of Gourna al-Gadida, near the Valleys of the Kings, Queens and Nobles in Luxor. The inhabitants of the existing village were tunnelling into the slopes near their houses and robbing the tombs. The artifacts that they found were then sold privately, or even worse, the gold was melted down and sold as crude ingots. After the complete removal and sale of a large stone bas-relief from one of the tombs came to the attention of the Department, it was decided to put an end to the destruction, and relocate the entire settlement. Fifty acres of agricultural land near the Nile was acquired from a local landowner by compulsory purchase as the site for the new village which was intended to rehouse seven thousand Gournii. Fathy recognized this meant moving

a complex network of blood and marital relations. This, together with their customs and taboos, their friendships and their disputes, a social organism delicately balanced, intimately integrated into the topography, to every wall and beam of the village. The whole society was going to be dismantled and reassembled in a new place.[1]

Gourna al-Gadida, with the Valley of the Kings visible in the background.

Opposite Gouache for New Gourna. Fathy combines Pharaonic perspective with architectural plans. Hathor, the fertility goddess represented by the cow, blesses the project. The sycamore tree, in the centre, the sign of Osiris, represents regeneration.

Fathy saw New Gourna not only as a large architectural commission, but also as a prototype that might provide an answer to the problem of housing the Egyptian peasant in a safe, sanitary and inexpensive way. He found the village to be generally divided into five tribes within four distinct zones on the hillside, with every tribe specifically separated into *badanas*, or family groupings, each led by a sheikh or patriarch.

Fathy determined to retain this four-part division in the new village:

> This layout of the main streets separated the four 'quarters' of the village. In each of these quarters was to be housed one of the main tribal groups of Old Gourna. ... The broad streets separating the quarters were intended as main traffic routes connecting all the public buildings and meeting in the square. To ensure good ventilation and isolation of the blocks of houses, as well as to facilitate movement and to mark off the quarters, these streets were at least 10 metres wide. By contrast, the streets giving access to the semiprivate squares ... of the different *badanas* were made deliberately narrow – no more than 6 metres wide – to provide shade and a feeling of intimacy, and included many corners and bends, so as to discourage strangers from using them as thoroughfares. ... I did not give the streets this crooked plan simply to make them quaint or because of some love for the Middle Ages. If I had adopted a regular plan like a gridiron, then the houses would have been forced into a uniform design too.[2]

Speaking about the individual houses in particular, he said:

> In Gourna, by compelling myself to fit the houses, which varied in size according to the area of the original houses they were replacing, into a variety of irregular plots, and by being ready to vary the plan of each to suit the people who would live in

it, I made sure that I should think carefully about the design of each one, avoid the trap of adding variety without purpose... My irregular plan made for variety and originality in design, for constant visual interest, and precluded the building of those boring ranks of identical dwellings that are often considered to be all that the poor deserve.[3]

Such attention to the individual concerns and personalities of the inhabitants of a housing group was

certainly novel at this time, when European architects were putting forward extremely regimented proposals, such as can be seen in the Weissenhof-Seidlung exhibition organized by Ludwig Mies van der Rohe in Stuttgart in 1922, that was soon to become the norm for the Modern movement.

Because of the need to establish an entirely new economy and lifestyle for the villagers, based on agricultural and crafts-based pursuits rather than excavation, the core of the community revolves around a market on the one hand and a *khan* (an inn for

Plan of New Gourna showing the constructed area, approximately one fifth of what was originally planned. The market is the area planted with trees at the top left. Fathy's house is just left of centre, almost enclosed by two irregularly shaped blocks. To the right of centre, enclosing a long courtyard, is the *khan* (market). Below right is the mosque. The theatre is on the far right.

travellers) on the other. While the market was intended for the sale and shipment of the agricultural produce taken from the fields surrounding the town, the *khan* was designed for the promotion of traditional crafts that it was hoped would be bought by the crowds of tourists that were expected to enter the main square from the road to the Valley of the Kings and Queens,

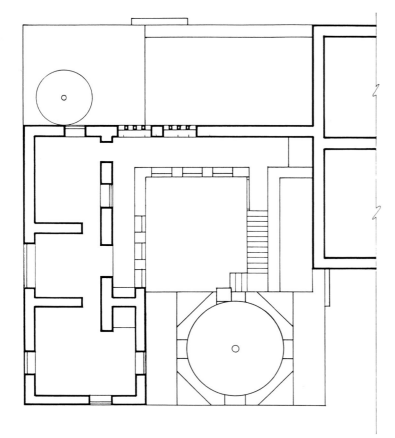

Fathy's field house at New Gourna. The simplicity of the plan reflects the house's basic, functional design.

nearly five kilometres away. Like New Gourna itself, the *khan* was intended as a model, and represented a re-creation of the crafts halls of the past where masters taught the mysteries of their profession to their apprentices. More than just a line of shops, the form of the *khan* also recalls the caravanserai of medieval Cairo, into which travelling merchants entered through a guarded portal leading into a large central court. After unloading their goods in the court, the merchants could retire for the night in the rooms provided there, turning the caravanserai into something closely resembling a hotel. Fathy's *khan* was provided with rooms for long-term stay in which he thought masters of various crafts would stay until they could successfully transfer their knowledge to the people of the village. The crafts that the townspeople produced would then be sold in the domed cubicles facing onto the main square, which would have given that part of the town the flavour of the *suqs* or bazaars so common to the small villages through the countryside near Gourna.

Fathy's own field office is located directly opposite to the diagonal cut that separates the crafts area from the rooms of the *khan*, to the northeast of that opening. Located in the centre of the neighbourhood which he created there, this charming house, which is still occasionally used by researchers coming to visit the village today, allowed the architect to be in the middle of the action during the construction process. He also delighted in using the house to entertain important guests from Cairo, as it has several rooms and a spacious *qa'a* overlooking a small central courtyard.

References have been made in the past to the architect's failure to provide for running water in the houses here. He explained his concern about disrupting

the pattern followed throughout rural Egypt of using a communal well. He was also aware of the subtle social effects that such a change would have, such as removing the only opportunity that young girls of marriageable age might have of being seen by prospective husbands who gather to watch the parade to the well each day. Centralized water sources were placed, instead, in the middle of each neighbourhood, such as the one near his field office at the corner of the *khan*.

Fathy's field house, New Gourna.

Left The chimney above the courtyard in front of the dome is evidence of the need to heat the *qa'a* during very cold nights.

Right The house overlooks the street (**above**); the main entrance (**below**), which opens into the courtyard, is modest and unassuming.

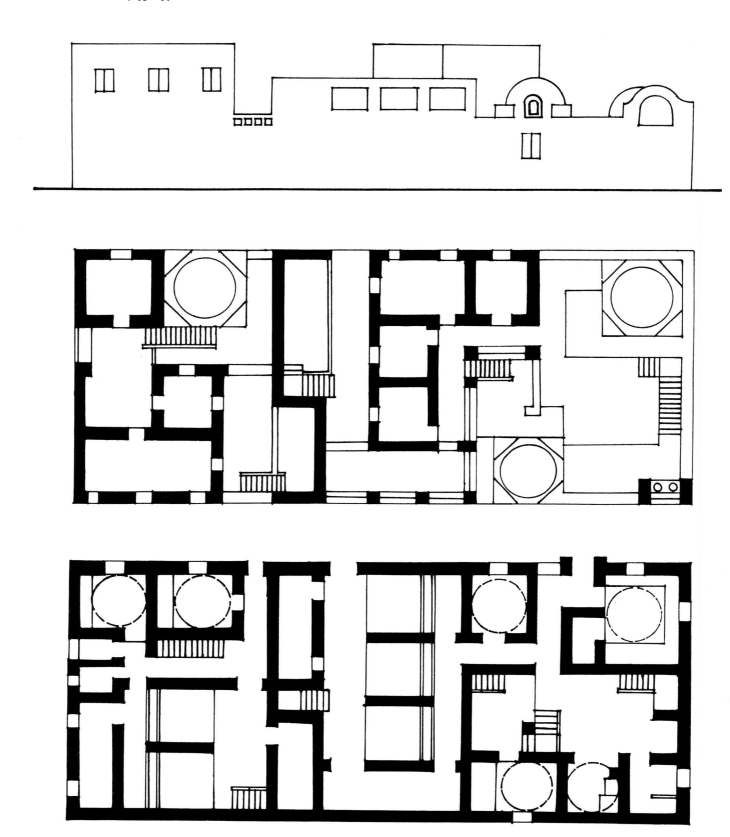

Elevation and plans of typical housing block for New Gourna. On the ground floor (**bottom**) three livestock stalls can be seen in the centre of the building, connecting with the family's living area, in accordance with local practice.

The commercial, agrarian counterpart of the *khan* is located at the opposite end of the street that curves away from it to the east. Fathy chose this location because of a narrow-gauge railroad track nearby. This railroad, which was built during the reign of Muhammad Ali, was part of one of the first such systems in the Middle East, and was intended for the shipment of sugar cane and cotton to refineries and markets in Cairo. The architect saw it as a logical commercial entrance to the village that would complement the tourist approach by road.

The wide open market in between was designed to accommodate the raucous buying and selling of livestock and produce that is so common in towns like Idfu and Isna nearby, and would certainly make this area a thriving hub of activity. Rows of trees were to provide a green canopy under which the sellers would spread their goods, and wide aisles were provided between them for the buyers to walk along. Fathy hoped that agricultural production would be extensive enough at some point to allow surplus goods to be sold in other villages down the line, or even in Cairo itself, and the amount of land allocated to New Gourna certainly supports this prediction.

In a famous series of lectures given at al-Azhar University in 1967, almost exactly twenty years after work on New Gourna had stopped, Fathy spoke passionately about the dangers inherent in changing urban patterns, and the great responsibility that planners assume when they undertake to create a town from the very beginning. In one of these lectures, called 'What is a City?', he elaborated in great detail upon many ideas that were later echoed by urban planner Jacqueline Tyrwhitt, whom he had come to

know at the Ekistics Centre in Athens. Both his lecture, and Tyrwhitt's book *Human Identity in the Urban Environment*, focus on what she has called the need for a 'human-scale intermediary' in towns and cities, and the importance of allowing for gradual, rather than traumatic, changes in scale from one part to another. As Fathy has described this in his lecture:

When planning a city one has to consider the man who is being planned for. Imagine him roving around the streets, squares and open spaces and try to create a harmony in the visual images he is going to look at, full of nice surprises without boring him or overwhelming him with details that make him uneasy. Speak to his feelings using all the forms of planning that create strong impressions and changes of mood as well as a feeling of expansion; an increasing generalization that begins when he goes from his house to the side street, and then to the main street, the square and finally to the centre of town in a graduation of scales that is something like a crescendo in music. The opposite should happen when this man comes back home from the centre of town – decrescendo.[4]

His awareness of these concerns, which are now being debated by those involved in urban rebuilding, once again show his remarkable prescience; and consideration of New Gourna, as well as his lectures and writings, should sufficiently answer those who claim that Fathy has never been interested in urban problems.

Gouache of the mosque at New Gourna. While borrowing traditional Nubian forms, Fathy balances the minaret with a dome. The extension at the far left houses the ablution area. The tree growing in the courtyard occupies the sacred centre of the temple, representing nature as the centre of life.

The mosque at New Gourna, as was once traditionally the case, was one of the first buildings to be constructed, and unlike the other buildings finally completed nearby, it has been lovingly maintained and appears much the same today as it must have in 1945. Many of Fathy's detailed surveys of the Nubian mosques close to Aswan still survive and bear evocative reminders of this building. The massive battered walls, the dramatic triangular stair to a tripartite minaret, and the prominent dome over the main prayer space are all recurrent themes in these Nubian mosques and occur in various permutations in all of the architect's survey drawings of them; but none have exactly the same massing as his design. With his characteristically fresh sense of composition, Fathy has taken these same strong forms and arranged them in such a way that they perfectly counterbalance each other along the horizontal datum line he sets up with the top of the mosque wall. Because of its prominent position directly opposite the only highway that leads from the Nile embankment to the Valley of the Kings and Queens nearly five kilometres away, as well as from the main gateway into the main square of New Gourna from that highway, this elevation was carefully designed both to symbolize the spiritual values inherent in the mosque and to introduce those entering through the main gateway to the ideals embodied in the community itself. The main dome, which anchors the right-hand side of this elevation, is the most venerable of the spiritual symbols used, having religious associations that even predate the use of the minaret itself in the sacred architecture of Islam.

As a clue to his approach to the dome over the prayer space in the New Gourna mosque, Fathy wrote:

69

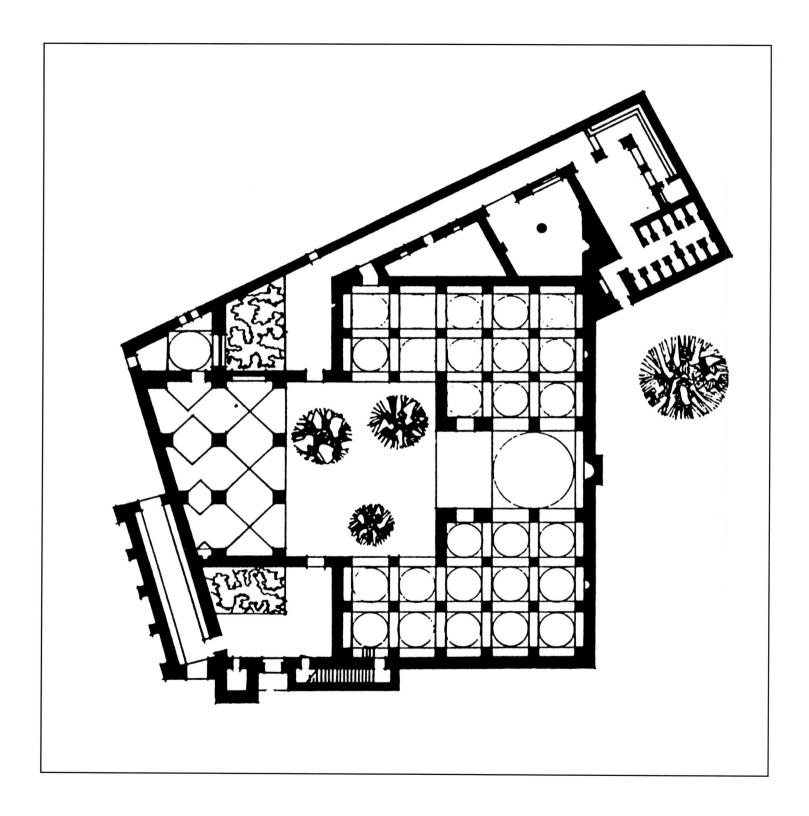

Plan of the mosque at New Gourna. Fathy corrected the original site plan, so that it faced Mecca. This had the effect of adding a dynamic quality to the whole plan. The minaret is at the bottom left-hand corner. The dome is to the right of the central courtyard.

in Islamic architecture, the symbol of the dome is different from the Byzantine according to the faith. The sanctuary being outside its walls, there in Mecca, the mosque is not an isolated microcosm complete in itself. 'It is a clean and quiet place for the prayers under the sky. If the worshippers were to be protected from the elements under a roof, this roof should not cut them off from the holiness of the sky and the same symbol of the dome was used in certain parts, but here, the Byzantine dome was substituted with the Sassanian dome on squinches in which the square is transformed into an octagon and the octagon into the circle expressing movement upwards with the eight sides of the octagon symbolizing the eight angels carrying the throne of God.[5]

If the hemispherical form of the dome symbolizes the replication of the sky vault on earth, the vertical emphasis of the minaret, which counters the dome here on the left-hand side of the elevation, points toward heaven itself. Fathy explains his idea for this vertical emphasis:

The minaret should be placed in a position to make a comprehensive and aesthetic composition with the dome, both being elements that go above the building, playing a major role in defining its silhouette against the sky. The dome as seen looking upwards from inside expresses the sky, but seen from the exterior, it looks like a shell structure bending downwards, needing the minaret in the composition to correct this effect.[6]

Jonathan Bloom, Professor of Architecture at Harvard University, in a paper delivered at a meeting of the North American Historians of Islamic Art in Washington, D.C. in 1981, spoke about five Fatimid minarets in Upper Egypt, and also noted that the minaret in general does not appear in mosque design in the early Islamic period. Tracing the etymology of the Arabic word *manara*, Bloom notes that this literally means the place of *nur*, or light, and that rather than being the place from which the call to prayer was given, the minaret may have originated as a tower in which a light was placed to mark the main pilgrimage road from Kufa to Mecca. All five were built between 1077 and 1082 in a similar vernacular style that includes the use of mud brick as a building material, and all five are divided into three distinct parts: square base, cylindrical central shaft and domed cap. That division is identifiable in other examples contemporary with them, across the Red Sea in the Hijaz region of Arabia, which would definitely establish that Fathy's minaret has local as well as pan-Islamic associations. Bloom states that the minaret did not become an accepted part of the mosque typology until the Abbasid period, somewhere between 750 and 1258, and that minarets were certainly not common in the mosques that the Fatimids built in Cairo until 1150. This theory supports the idea that these five examples were of vernacular and not Fatimid origin and design.

In his own study of mosque architecture, Fathy analyses the form of the minaret in great detail, paying special attention to the ways in which certain compositional devices have been used in the most well known examples of the past to enhance a desirable impression of verticality. Applying mathematical rules

NEW GOURNA: 1945-47

Below and right Beneath the main dome, New Gourna mosque. The recesses of the stepped squinches (**below**), which resolve the square form with the round base of the dome, provide decorative sculptural forms inside.

Opposite, above New Gourna mosque, showing the roof of the hypostyle prayer area, with domes built above square column bays. It was intended that the fields in the background should provide the source of the community's agricultural economy.

Opposite, below left The building's stone foundation is visible where it has been exposed at the bottom of the near corner. Generally the mosque has lasted well, with good maintenance and annual replastering in mud.

Opposite, below right The influence of the typical Nubian mosque form is clearly visible in profile.

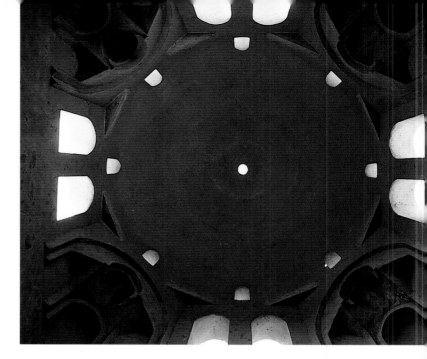

of logarithmic progression to each of the examples he uses, he systematically shows how each tower is divided into sections and how these sections, in turn, are rhythmically shortened toward the top to create a harmonious acceleration, as the eye moves from the base upwards.

Taken as a whole, the main facade of the New Gourna mosque, while appearing simple, uses a very deliberate and sophisticated kind of iconography, combining several architectural elements that each have complex historical connotations. At one level, those connotations are regional, and Nubian, while at another, they transcend local tradition to make a connection with the formation of Islamic identity itself. Spatially, the mosque continues this kind of duality, with a prayer area wrapped around an inner courtyard that has three entrances. The first of these is intended for those who have performed the necessary ablutions in their homes before coming to the mosque, and are already clean. As with the design of the minaret, the architect's intention here was to also create an impression of aspiration in the form, by using a high, rounded top on the door frame, which is deeply inscribed into the surface of the thick mosque wall. This inscription shows the negative outline of the minaret in miniature, with a small semi-circular cut taken out of the top of the arch to mimic the rounded cap of the tower next to it. The door itself, which is deeply recessed into the wall, is painted in the particular shade of green usually associated with the heavenly paradise mentioned in the Qur'an.

In the best tradition of such well known mosques as that of Sultan Hassan in Cairo, where each worshipper is led from the main entrance along

Opposite and above The heavy massing of the mud-brick walls in New Gourna and the use of groin vaults, such as these near the market place, recall Romanesque architecture. Openwork masonry screens provide ventilation.

a circuitous pathway into the interior court, because of the adjustments that are necessary between the prerequisites of street direction on the one hand, and the orientation of the *qibla* (direction of prayer) toward Mecca on the other, Fathy introduces a *magaz*, or offset entry, into his own plan to deal with this discrepancy (p. 70). In addition to helping make this re-orientation possible, the *magaz* also acts as a valve between the large public square outside and the quiet sanctity of the interior and prepares the worshipper for prayer. As in the residential counterparts that Fathy has studied in medieval Cairo, this *magaz* is also provided with a *mastaba*, or step, that is increased in scale here to be used for sitting, making this a social space where people may gather after prayers to talk.

A long vaulted passage running along the outside wall on the left, or 'unclean' side of the main entrance, leads those who have not yet washed to a second doorway in the back of the mosque, along another walled enclosure into the ablutionary. This vaulted passage, which is lined with a row of buttresses that serve to reinforce it visually, rather than structurally, is skewed to align with a group of houses there were planned to be next to it, and because the mosque was the first building to be built in the village, the angle used was established by aesthetic considerations rather than a pre-existing condition. The same may be said for the long ablutionary wall at the rear of the building, and both of these deliberately spiral out from the linear axis of the prayer area in a way that was obviously intended to create a dynamic divergence of directions in the village plan, beginning at the mosque in the centre. This divergence is not as obvious when looking at the portion of the village that was actually built, but the original master plan reveals this intention very clearly. In it, the mosque has been positioned at the centre of the entire village, with streets radiating out from it towards other major institutions such as the boys' and girls' schools and the market that serve as anchors for each side of the perimeter. Rather than being at the heart of the village today, as intended, the mosque is now completely isolated, surrounded only by the space which should have been occupied by the houses that would have framed it, and looking out over fields that were to provide a new economic base for the community.

In his wish to keep tradition alive, and to provide a place for visitors and townspeople alike to see authentic rituals, Fathy designed an open-air *palestra* or fighting stage to be located near the gateway of the New Gourna public square, with a permanent crafts exhibition and hotel separating it from the main road on one side and the administrative offices of the mayor, and his private residence, on the other. Sa'idi 'stick

fighting', which looks so innocent and amusing when rehearsed for public consumption, is in reality a deadly martial art that has evolved within a rural culture. Such fighting, which is still performed, was used in the past to settle personal or tribal disputes, and even though it is now more sedate than it once was, it can still result in broken bones or even fatality. In spite of the real danger involved, it is considered as much an art form as the oriental martial disciplines. Fathy later wrote:

> Situated right on the square, the theatre is equipped with all of the facilities needed for folklorique performances, singing, conferences, film projection, and many different kinds of gatherings. The stick-fencing championships are also contested here. Therefore these last structures progressively draw one into the life of this new village and the interests of the people, and reveal their devotion to the communal task of making a living in order to prosper as much as possible.[7]

Much to the architect's credit, he was not only deeply concerned that all of the inhabitants of Gourna al-Gadida could be accommodated in the new village he was designing for them, but was also trying his utmost to ensure that it would take root, because this crucial transition represented nothing less than an

New Gourna was to be the realization of Fathy's dream of a utopian community, unified with nature, as in this gouache (**opposite**) exhibited in Mansuriya in 1937. The boys' school (**above**) has now disappeared, like so much of what was built, destroyed by disuse and neglect.

entire change in the living patterns of seven thousand people. While another designer might have simply been content with a functional arrangement of spaces sufficient to answer programmatic requirements, Fathy looked deeper into all of the possibilities that this new site offered to his reluctant clients. His relationship with them gradually changed from open hostility on their part to sincere friendliness, according to his memoirs. The adherence and co-operation he thought he observed may have been more wishful thinking than

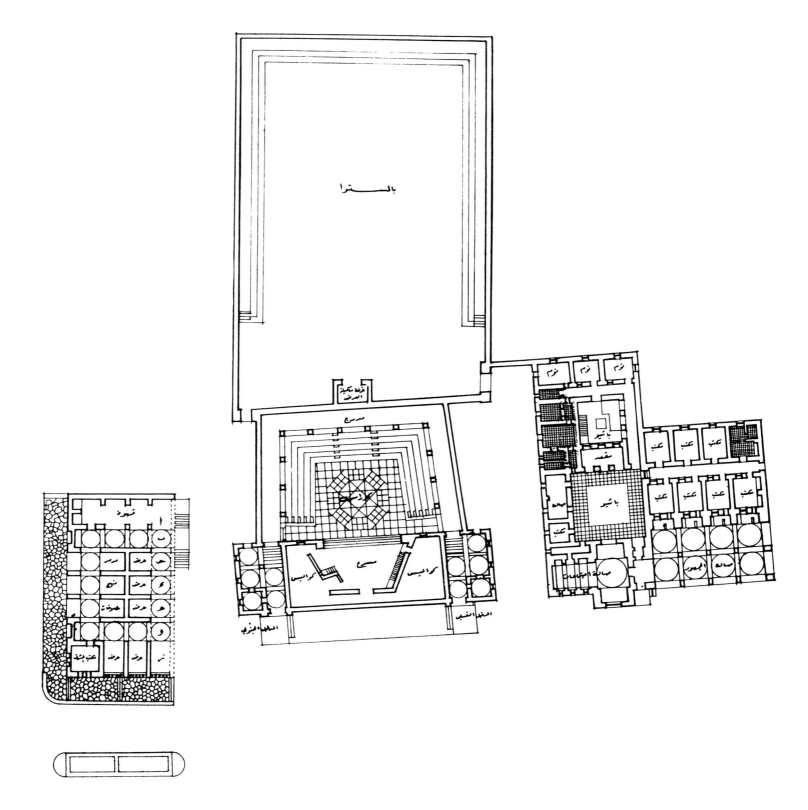

Plan of the theatre at New Gourna. The theatre is divided into two parts: shown in the lower half of the plan, the built-in stage set with closely arranged seating; in the upper part, a larger area for Sa'idi stick-fighting.

reality as several attempts at sabotage were later to prove, but his wish to see the village flourish was sincere, and he tried every design tactic within principle to ensure its success.

Each day thousands of tourists take the ferry across the Nile from Luxor to the west bank of the river to see the tombs in the Valleys of the Kings, Queens and Nobles about five kilometres inland, and travel there by taxi, mini-bus, tour bus, bicycle, donkey or on foot along the single, narrow, two-lane road. Fathy looked at that road and the potential customers on it as one of the main lifelines of the new village, and an endless source of legal business transactions in the future. Like any good shopkeeper, he decided to locate his wares right near the main lines of traffic, in an open-air structure that would show them off to best effect and tempt people to stop. His permanent crafts exhibition hall was intended as a signboard to promote sales and is surrounded by the only hard stone paving in the entire project in anticipation of the crowds that he thought would want to visit.

Various markets similar to this one now exist at several places along the road to the Valley, selling alabaster and other local crafts. Fathy's idea was to introduce the entire gamut of crafts into the village, which would ensure a wider market and more interest from the tourists. By doing so, he also hoped to save many of these local crafts from extinction. His particular use of *mashrabiya* (wooden latticework screens), wooden doors and plaster-and-glass *kamariyya* windows in all of his own residential projects have already had a considerable impact upon the vitality of these trade skills in Cairo.

The hotel portion of the crafts exposition was also intended for visitors who wanted to see more of the village, and was located in a suitably segregated part of the site, screened off from the public square and the houses of the villagers by the high walls of the theatre. As it is shown only on some plans produced during the proposal stage, it seems there was a certain ambivalence about including this particular building at all.

The theatre, which inflects slightly to one side to guide people around and into the main square, actually seems to make the physical gesture of welcome that the architect has spoken about, and its prominent double-gated facade is an important part of this side of the plaza. Fathy was fond of theatre, and even wrote a play for the local children to make them aware of the dangers of bilharzia. The seating is designed on wide low ledges that are accessible from a vine-covered colonnade that runs around behind them. An arrangement of free-standing screens, and the stairs attached to them, were meant to accommodate a wide variety of productions, and today stand in De Chirico-like abstraction, awaiting the various scenes to be put on in front of them. The westerly orientation of both the theatre and the *palestra* ensures that they receive the rich, golden light of the late afternoon sun even after it has gone below the parapet, and the long shadows cast by the pergola arcade and screens create a performance of their own at that time of the day. Having fallen into disrepair through lack of use and proper maintenance, the theatre has recently been restored by several of Fathy's followers and students, with the same construction techniques that were originally used to build it. The two imposing doors that lead up to its gallery, however, are still always locked, and the

The theatre at New Gourna, with its own permanent built-in set, has recently been restored by a group of Fathy's friends and followers. Fathy himself wrote several plays, some of which were intended to be performed here.

performance of plays like Fathy's own *The Tale of the Mashrabiya* that he hoped would help one culture to understand another, have yet to take place here.

The mayor's house and offices, which are the third component of this group of buildings, symbolically and physically mediate between those functions related to visitors and the houses of the village nearby. As in his private houses, Fathy uses a *qa'a* as a reception area here for those waiting for access to the offices connected to it. These offices actually fall into two separate categories, with those of higher rank placed facing inward along a corridor that has only a single access from one side of the square courtyard in the middle of the building. Residential spaces are placed on the far side of this courtyard, and also relate to a second, smaller court, in order to remain totally private from the office area. In a small detail that is typical of Fathy's consistent inventiveness, an end wall of the mayor's house extends out to engage the far jamb of the main doorway into the *palestra*, thus working along with the angled wall of the theatre to form a clear, comfortable and perfectly proportioned entry into that arena.

These and several of the other public buildings here have drawn criticism that rather than drawing visitors into the life of this new village, as Fathy claimed they would, these institutions have instead been one of the main reasons for its death. Questioning the appropriateness of such additions as a theatre, gymnasium, hotel, *khan*, Turkish bath and Coptic church to what was supposed simply to have been an improved version of a typical rural Egyptian village, these critics have charged Fathy with romanticism and a lack of real understanding of the traditional customs and lifestyle of the *fellahin*.

Fathy's description in *Architecture for the Poor* of the hindrance and callousness that he faced from both the Department of Antiquities and the Gournii themselves should suffice to remind critics of the real cause of the failure of this project. Fathy was undoubtedly often a showman, as is obvious in the planning of his 'Fête de Gourna' held in the theatre there soon after its completion. Beautiful posters celebrating this Fête were hung on the stark outer wall of the theatre that night, and important guests coming in from Cairo were shown to their seats by torchlight, to the accompaniment of drums. While such gestures may seem frivolous, in the light of the higher purpose of the village, they also served a political end in allowing the architect to consolidate support for the project.

Egypt has been layered with so many cultures over time that it would be difficult to separate out what is and is not Egyptian in New Gourna. The concept of a gymnasium, for example, is Greek in origin, and both this and the theatre were conspicuously used by Alexander the Great in the areas that he conquered to ensure that Greek social customs would take hold and flourish. Ptolemy, as one of his successors, claimed Egypt as his kingdom upon Alexander's death, and the dynasty that he created there has since become inextricably identified with the country in the public consciousness, particularly in the person of Cleopatra, who was its last sovereign. In his zeal to put New Gourna on a viable economic footing, Fathy may have overrated the value of such institutions and their role in his design, just as he over-scaled the main square to accept the flood of tourists that he hoped would visit there.

Such debate about his supposedly unrealistic romanticism tends to obscure the significance of his achievement at New Gourna, and although the village as it stands today is only a small portion of what was ultimately planned, that achievement is undeniably impressive. Most of the houses that were finished are now occupied, although not by the Gournii, who have gone back to their original hillside and old way of life. Few changes have been made to those houses in the interim, and with the exception of some animal pens that have been built in front of several of the buildings, as well as some filled-in windows and doors and bad maintenance, Fathy's design has remained intact.

There is no question that he managed to capture the true spirit of the people themselves:

Being faithful to a style, in the way I mean it, does not mean the reverent reproductions of other people's creation. It is not enough to copy even the very best buildings of another generation or another locality. The method of building may be used, but you must strip from this method all the

Fathy's gouache for his play *The Tale of the Mashrabiya*, which he described as 'a kind of architectural fable'. The handcrafted *mashrabiya* (wooden latticework screen) represents the passing on of traditional skills from generation to generation. The play warns against the loss of traditional architecture. The classical Arabic text at the top and bottom of the miniature records a conversation between two characters symbolically named Mushtaq (yearning) and Nadim (friend):

On the top:
MUSHTAQ: Look! The sun is breaking through the clouds. The rose is in blossom, and the bee is taking its nectar. God, who is the Creator of the Universe, be praised.

NADIM: Look! The bee is transmitting its message of love to the flourishing rose, at the end of the garden, which is longing to receive it.

MUSHTAQ: The rose is also giving up its nectar generously, and as it does, life goes on and its cycle is completed. The bee holds the rose in its arms.

On the bottom:
MUSHTAQ: I will never be able to forget this *mashrabiya*. Its ornament is like a melody from a lute.

NADIM: Listen! Don't you hear the music?

MUSHTAQ: How odd! I always thought that this silent house was uninhabited. When I look at the *mashrabiya*, I also feel as if it is music.

NADIM: This house really does not look as if it is inhabited. No one passing by would know whether the owners live here or are far away.

MUSHTAQ: But who are they?

NADIM: They are the family of a prince. People have many different ideas about where this prince comes from. Persians say he is from Isphahan, Arabs say he is from al-Musel and Syrians say he is from Damascus.

MUSHTAQ: His sophisticated taste is evidence of his noble descent. If he has been able to attain such a high degree of harmony on the outside of this house, imagine what it must look like on the inside.

substance of particular character and detail, and drive out from your mind the picture of the houses that so beautifully fulfilled your desires. You must start right from the beginning, letting your new buildings grow from the daily lives of the people who will live in them, shaping the houses to the measure of the people's songs, weaving the patterns of a village as if on the village looms, mindful of the trees and the crops that will grow there, respectful to the skyline and humble before the seasons. There must be neither faked tradition nor faked modernity, but an architecture that will be the visible and permanent expression of the character of a community. But this would mean nothing less than a whole new architecture.[8]

New Gourna, undoubtedly Fathy's best-known project, is significant because it was his first officially sanctioned opportunity to test his radical ideas on a large scale. It failed because its intended inhabitants were reluctant to relocate and sabotaged the project, and powerful rivals lobbied government ministries, particularly the Ministry of Culture, to stop it. Wartime shortages and political upheaval also contributed to its cancellation.

It is generally assumed that Fathy somehow got it wrong, that his adopted system of typologies was misdirected, and that this was the reason why the Gournii did not take up residence. While the appropriateness of his regeneration of typologies in general may be questioned, this is not why work on New Gourna stopped, or why the town was unoccupied.

Mashrabiya, or wooden latticework screen. The wooden elements are rounded to deflect glare, providing no reflective flat surfaces. The wood absorbs moisture, creating a cooling effect as the air passes through.

A gouache (p. 82), intended as a companion piece to Fathy's play *The Tale of the Mashrabiya*, is one of the most charming that he painted, as well as one of the most technically accomplished. Executed in the style of a Persian miniature, it was also meant to serve as a guide for the stage set that might be used for his play, and bears a strong resemblance to the arrangement of the theatre he had designed for New Gourna.

Fathy described his play as 'a kind of architectural fable'. It describes the passing on from generation to generation of traditions, traditional architecture, and especially crafts, which he saw as being threatened. The *mashrabiya* is the symbol of an endangered craft, and until the recent crafts renaissance that Fathy himself helped to initiate, it had fallen into disuse and was no longer appreciated.

The *mashrabiya* is an appropriate symbol on several levels, because it evolved for social as well as environmental reasons. The form of the *mashrabiya* evolved from a simple, flat perforated wooden screen into an elegant, bracketed projection, which would allow its occupants to sit inside. Traditionally used on both the outer and inner walls of the house in the past, its primary social function was to prevent the women of the family from being seen by strangers, by providing a screen that would allow them to look down into the street below, or into the courtyard, or *qa'a* from the floor above without being seen. It therefore became an architectural expression of a cultural necessity. Fathy described the practical function of the design, in a lecture at the School of Fine Arts in Cairo:

The *mashrabiya* reduces the reflected heat and the solar radiation and allows air to pass through freely. Making the balusters round helps to diffuse light and shade and prevents the glare that can occur due to the contrast between their edges and the light coming through the spaces between them. If these balusters were square or rectangular in section, they would create glare because of the contrast of light and shade at the hard edge. From the bottom of the *mashrabiya* up to eye-level the spaces between the balusters gradually become smaller and the pattern narrower in order to prevent glare, and above eye-level the spaces become larger and the pattern wider to allow more light to enter the upper parts of the rooms in the *qa'a*. Thus they obtained enough light indoors without glare occurring at eye-level.[9]

Omar el-Farouk, who was once a student of Hassan Fathy and now has his own practice in Maadi, outside Cairo, has done exhaustive research on the history and function of the *mashrabiya*. He found that the screens, in addition to providing privacy, cutting down glare and allowing natural ventilation, also had hygroscopic properties: the wooden balusters retain humidity of the air that passes through them. On every level, the *mashrabiya* proves, as Fathy states, that 'culture is the unique human response of man to his environment in his attempt to answer both physical and spiritual needs.'

Omar el-Farouk has spoken of the irony that he himself had to travel to London to research a subject that should have been available in his own country. Fathy's play illustrates this loss of interest in the traditions of the past in a scene in which two Nubian men argue about which side of a *kilim* (carpet) should face upwards. By depicting them as being distrustful of

The Parliament of the Pharaohs, gouache. This encyclopaedic presentation of ancient symbols is related to the most stable period of Egyptian history.

instincts which happen to be correct, Fathy reflects on local traditions which are felt to be inferior and become lost. In his 'fable,' anyone wishing to find the few surviving *mashrabiya* had to become resigned to searching through junkyards, where the screens were being broken up and sold for use in tables, chairs and mirror frames, or were being passed off to movie producers who wanted to paint them gold or white and use them as part of the background in exotic, oriental scenes. *The Tale of the Mashrabiya* relates to basic questions of cultural identity and may quite possibly be intended to be autobiographical.

One year after the construction of the village of New Gourna had stopped, Fathy published an unusual story called 'Le Pays d'Utopie' in *La Revue du Caire*. It depicts a wise man and a beautiful woman who set out in search of truth and a perfect place to live. Their experience of modern urban life, with skyscrapers, apartment living and increasing dependence on the machine, highlights the utopian ideal they eventually find – an old house built long ago whose traditional architecture embodies humanistic values and harmony with community, environment and nature. 'Le Pays d'Utopie' ends with the disillusioned couple, like Fathy himself, leaving the paradise of the green valley, unable to realize the dream promised by the Ancient Book. The fable is obviously an allegory of his own bitter experience at New Gourna and reveals a side of him that *Architecture for the Poor*, for all its skill, never does. His hopes for that village, and the pain that he felt in not being able to achieve them, are expressed through a thin veil of metaphor. The similarity between his gouache of New Gourna (p. 60) and his sketch of the green valley, one of three which accompany the story,

indicate a graphic wish for a return to the agricultural prosperity of the past, that would allow its people to put aside avarice and live in harmony with the land, rather than tunnelling into it. This wish is confirmed by the presence of the goddess Hathor, shown as a cow:

> The cow gives milk, just as the sky gives life to the earth…if it weren't for the humidity in the atmosphere there would be no life on earth. It is the water falling from heaven that creates all plant life and sustains all human and animal life, which is why the Pharaohs had a goddess of the sky, called Hathor.[10]

Fathy's gouache of New Gourna expresses his empathy with both the living conditions and status of the client. He stressed that he tried to approach the design of New Gourna not as a city dweller, but as one of the villagers, in trying to anticipate their needs. Since Muhammad Ali requisitioned all of the land of Egypt when he came to power in the nineteenth century, the *fellah* (peasant) has not been able to own his house or property and his connection with the land has effectively been broken. Prior to having been relegated to tenancy, however, Fathy noted that the *fellahin* were once proud of their houses and tried to express their own individuality in their design; but with the advent of large landholdings distributed to royal favourites, decisions began to be made on a purely economic basis, and personal pride of ownership disappeared. The Nubians, he added, were beyond central authority and therefore escaped such domination, so that the creativity that was evident in their houses, until their homeland was destroyed by the Aswan High Dam in

1960, indicates what might have existed throughout Egypt and testifies to the obvious advantages of self-ownership. Fathy wrote:

> The Egyptian peasant has lived in this new environment deprived of Beauty. One hundred and fifty years have passed and the peasant has become accustomed to mediocrity; moreover, he has lost faith in any assistance that might come from the city. Thus it was difficult for the peasant in Gourna to believe that a city architect would be interested in him and would want to treat him like the home owner he used to be. Besides, the misery in which he had lived had made him change his values and…therefore Gourna was an attempt to restore aesthetic qualities to the world of the peasantry.[11]

The archaeologist R. A. Schwaller de Lubicz, a friend of Fathy's, focused on the mathematical and astrological systems that were developed by the Ancient Egyptians, and the way that they were reflected in their architecture. In his exhaustive study of these relationships, *The Temple in Man*, he put forward the hypothesis that the Pharaonic Temple itself was divided anthropologically into three distinct parts based on the legs, thorax and head of the human body. De Lubicz's theories greatly impressed Fathy, who consequently began to look more deeply into these mathematical relationships and layered them over the spatial and structural links he had already begun to form with the past. De Lubicz, among others, pointed out that the Egyptians were among the first civilizations to develop a systematic numerical ratio for the artistic

depiction of form, and that these mathematical ratios, which had their basis in the empirical astrological observations that became necessary to predict the exact time of the Nile flood, then carried over into their monumental architecture.

A drawing on papyrus (p. 87), which was done by Fathy sometime during the realization of the New Gourna project, clearly conveys the idea of the agricultural gift of the Nile, which provides the dominant horizon line on its upper border. Entitled *The Parliament of the Pharaohs*, it represents an imaginary meeting between the Kings of the Upper and Lower Egypt. Since a parliament, as such, obviously never existed at that time, the use of this concept in the title of the drawing shows Fathy's intention to present the idea of meeting, or joining together, and this intention is consistently reinforced at various levels by the images used in it.

The marsh at the bottom of the drawing, for example, which mirrors the curve of the Nile at the top, presents both the papyrus and the lotus plants, which were the heraldic symbols of the north and south respectively, and the hieroglyphic names inscribed inside the scarab-shaped area in the centre of the drawing are those of selected names in both regions. The kings shown in this meeting are probably intended to be generic, rather than actual individuals, because both wear the double crown, and carry a *sikham* rather than the royal sceptre, meaning that each stands between the gods and man, as Osiris did. Each is also shown beside a sacred sycamore tree, which like the twin turquoise sycamores mentioned in the *Book of the Dead*, flank the eastern gate of heaven used by the sun-god Ra on his morning journey across the sky.

Alternating rows of tamarisk trees and palms also surround the labyrinth in the centre of the drawing. Like the sycamore, the tamarisk has divine connotations because of its association with both Osiris and Isis, the principal deities in the Egyptian pantheon. Osiris was responsible for the introduction of organized agriculture into Egypt and is especially identified with the cultivation of barley and grapes. The palm trees, which alternate with the tamarisks here, provide an additional symbol of sustenance, with the doum-palm, one of the two main varieties that grow in Egypt, being especially identified with the upper part of the country.

The two gateways into the meeting place that Fathy has created are each protected by the *wedjet* eye of Horus which was felt to have apotropaic powers, and, with the hieroglyphic inscriptions below them, stand for a united Egypt. The other major entrance to the labyrinth is guarded by baboons, which, as representations of the god Thoth, were thought to count off each hour of the day and night; they stand for light and darkness. Since there are only eight shown here, they may stand for the Nile flood instead; the river usually overflowed its banks in July with the melting of the snow in the Ethiopian mountains, and receded in November, leaving eight months for planting. The scarab, which is at the heart of the entire composition, is one of the most powerful symbols of all, standing for renewal, as well as for the god Khepri, who, like the beetle, was thought to 'come forth from the centre of the earth'.

All of these complex references show that *The Parliament of the Pharaohs* was intended to have several levels of meaning. In the first of these, two unknown individuals came together in a representation of the joining of the two parts of the land. At another, more mystical level, Fathy intends the imaginary labyrinth and the gardens around it to stand for the annual renewal of Egypt itself; and by extension, for the endless cycle of life and death that was the obsessive concern of the ancient religion of that country. The constant references to renewal in that religion involved a cosmic order in which the Pharaoh was the embodiment of eternal life. Architecture, as the centre of Fathy's statement, becomes a part of this order, and since it is as ephemeral as the human beings that create it, and just as susceptible to destruction, the labyrinth becomes only a temporary reproduction of an eternal reality.

3
Further Testing of New Ideas: 1948–67

Fathy continued to develop the ideas that he had tested in the New Gourna design. Government bureaucracy had diminished the momentum that his idealism had generated but Fathy persisted in his belief that vernacular architecture could become the national style.

This view brought him into conflict with powerful adversaries. Osman Osman, who owned one of the largest construction conglomerates in Egypt and had powerful friends in government ministries, believed that, if left unchecked, Fathy's reliance on natural materials rather than steel and concrete would lead to lower building costs and lower profits for construction companies. He lobbied to block Fathy from government commissions and to prevent him from teaching.

Most of Fathy's projects after New Gourna were private and came about by social connections and private recommendation. His design for the Stopplaere house (1950), located in Luxor, came about as a result of his acquaintance with the archaeologist working in the area while Fathy was involved in New Gourna's construction. The house is an ingenious combination of a site office and private residence for the archaeological

Stopplaere house, Luxor, 1950. The stepped squinches of the dome give the building a distinctive silhouette, situated on a ridge at the entrance to the Valley of the Kings and Queens.

director. It is divided into two by a central courtyard, affording privacy for both areas. Its position at the top of a cliff at the entrance to the Valley of the Kings and Queens gives it a commanding presence that belies its small scale. The positioning was also pragmatic; archaeologists coming to the house at the end of the day to write their reports reached it along the top of the ridge on which it sits, which was at the same level as the excavations.

While Fathy's book about New Gourna describes the best-known community project of his career, it was by no means the only one. Shortly after work was stopped there in 1948, he was engaged by Hafiz Afifi Pasha to assist in improving staff facilities on his estate outside Cairo, Lulu'at al-Sahara (Pearl of the Sahara). This social housing community for agricultural workers was even more progressive in concept than New Gourna in its provision of large, airy living areas, good sanitation and ventilation. These improvements were to include housing for the tenant farmers, as well as an elementary school and a mosque, which remains one of Fathy's most accomplished buildings. The prayer hall is well proportioned, with a convenient relationship to the entrance courtyard and ablution area, and both areas are configured to conform comfortably to the site lines. The improvements were to be developed within the context of the existing estate, which contained the

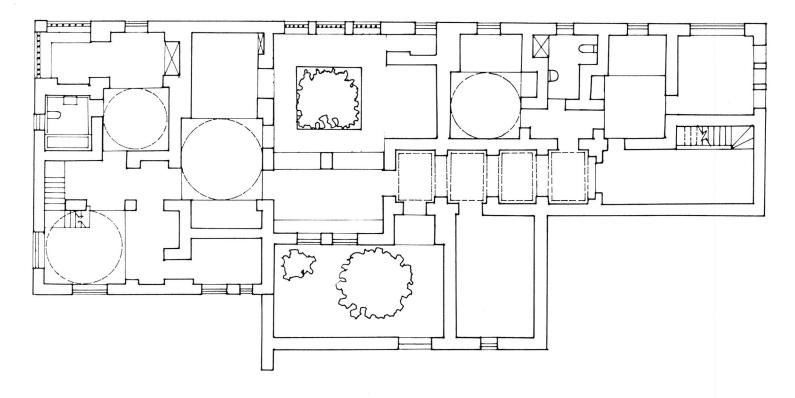

Plan of the Stopplaere house, Luxor. Different elements are accommodated with seeming ease around a central courtyard; an articulated gallery (shown by a row of four rooflights, centre right of the plan) joins the two sides of the house – the site office is on the left, the residential space on the right.

landlord's villa as well as a small medical facility, farm buildings and pigeon towers. The six duplex houses that he designed for the estate are each planned around an indirect passageway so that the units may be sited to form a wall around a large private interior courtyard for the use of the farm community. Stairways located in small courtyards attached to each unit lead to sleeping quarters above, oriented for view and ventilation. The farming community still operates, a testimony to its enduring design. As with all projects at this time, it is built entirely of mud brick using Fathy's typological language, and blends in with its surroundings: an undulating screen of palm trees against ploughed fields. The estate today remains a small green enclave near the creeping urban sprawl of Cairo, representing a unique example of an enlightened landowner's concern for the well-being of his employees.

The Ceramics Factory at Garagus was a smaller, crafts-based project which Fathy designed in 1950 for the Jesuit mission in Egypt as a means of assisting a rural village in the diversification of its agriculturally based economy. More alterations have been made here than in Lulu'at al-Sahara as a result of changing processes and expanding markets: the complex has been extended to allow for larger gas kilns. As a deceptively simple expression of the ceramic process, the design is very clear, with the spaces arranged sequentially from the arrival of the raw earth to the facility through to the glazing, firing and storage of the finished work. Fathy was guided by the dual concerns of natural ventilation and the best solar orientation for the work and studio spaces in this self-contained complex. As in Fathy's community designs, his scheme combines working, living, prayer and leisure. The plan, however, was greatly altered by the Jesuits during construction, and while the facility is still in operation today, the existing building does not match the organizational logic and restrained grace of the original concept.

Fathy was also engaged in various private projects in Cairo at this time. The Tusun Abu Gabal House (1947) in Cairo and the Eid House (1948) in Zagazig near Cairo reiterated Fathy's interest in vernacular forms. Fathy's marriage to Aziza Hassanein resulted in two commissions for this influential Cairo family. In 1946 he designed a mausoleum for his brother-in-law, Muhammad. Located at the edge of the City of the Dead, it remains a striking landmark seen by thousands of tourists from the Salah Salem highway on the way from the airport to central Cairo. In style (though not scale), it is indistinguishable from the Mamluk mausoleums built between the twelfth and fifteenth centuries.

In 1949 Fathy designed the Hassanein Villa, a house for his wife, Aziza, from whom he was separated at this time; the couple were married and lived together for only one year. The house was located alongside the Nile, and the roadside wall presented a shield to public view. The facade facing the river, however, had more openings, taking advantage of the view. This pattern, of a closed public side and open private side, is repeated many times in houses that followed, including the architect's own house (1971) in Sidi Krier near Alexandria. The Hassanein Villa was demolished because of road widening in 1951.

The Monastirli House (1950), located nearby, follows the same open–closed pattern though it uses a different style. Atiya Monastirli, the wife of the Egyptian Ambassador to Turkey, insisted on Turkish design, arranging for Hassan Fathy to stay in Istanbul for several months in order to study the houses along the Bosphorus. Cairo has a long history of Ottoman architecture, which Fathy studied in designing this house. The house bears no specific references to Turkish architecture, though there are elements of Egyptian Ottoman design, such as a court with shading pergola on the roof, and ornate stained glass windows interspersed between more conventional fenestration.

The house is in general more ornate and less vernacular in style than any others that the architect designed either at this time or later. It does indicate, however, a similar sensibility towards environmental concerns in its orientation of windows, the thickness of the walls to insulate against heat, maximizing the orientation of the building to harness river breezes and the use of a roof deck as an outdoor room during the warm evening hours. The Monastirli family had gained royal favour through excellence in military service, and they had been granted land to build a house on Roda island in the middle of the Nile, on which they built an entertainment pavilion or *salamlik*. Fathy based his design primarily on this existing building. It borrows

Stopplaere house, Luxor, showing the stepped squinches at the base of the dome.

the continuous large crown cornice on its formal two-storey face and the flat arch configuration used in a front entrance canopy and loggia arcade. The formal, processional entry into and through the house is masterfully conceived, leading from the front door into a domed central hall that overlooks the Nile. From this space, which is uncharacteristically detailed in heavy ornamental plaster, a stairway leads up to its open-air counterpart directly above, with the *umbilicus mundi* marked by a highly decorated marble fountain covered by an open wooden cupola.

Despite the official criticism of Fathy's work, he had friends in high places. In 1951 Fathy was made director of the school building department by the Egyptian Ministry of Education. While he was there he designed a prototype school at Fares near Luxor. The project was seen by Fathy as an opportunity to develop further his belief in the integration of environmental principles with cultural imperatives. In plan, the school is divided between administrative and communal facilities, including offices, a library, mosque and an assembly hall, and two ranks of classrooms facing each other across a courtyard that runs between them.

Because of the prohibitive cost of mechanical cooling and heating, Fathy predicated the entire design on natural ventilation, dividing each classroom into a square domed area for teaching connected to a rectangular vaulted space for ventilation. The rectangular space was originally intended to contain a pool of water to cool the air coming in through slots in the vault above it, and further ventilation was to be provided by operable windows in the classroom. Both methods have been subsequently altered by the users so that the classrooms that are still in operation do not

Above and opposite, below The sloping pier which extends from the main building indicates the demarcation line between the archaeological site office and Dr Stopplaere's private residential area.

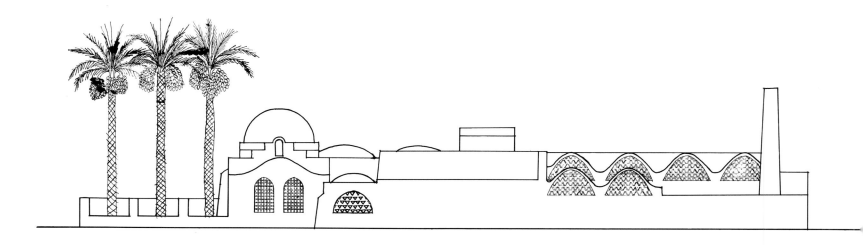

contain the water pool or casement windows. The design, however, is remarkably functional and environmentally comfortable. The domes and vaults clearly describe their function. The school design was repeated in Idfu but this second model was not well maintained and is now in a state of serious disrepair. The Fares model, however, perhaps because of closer ties to the community – located on a secluded island – remains in excellent condition and constant use.

The work on the schools at Fares and Idfu, and designs outside the country for the Chilean Nitrate Company and for prototypical housing units for refugees in Gaza, mark the end of this phase of Fathy's career in Egypt. Government criticisms published in the national press of the financial viability of the

Elevation of the Ceramics Factory, Garagus, 1950. Designed as an expression of the ceramic process, the space is arranged sequentially from the arrival of raw earth through to glazing, firing and storage of the finished work. Although much altered, the factory is still in operation.

Right Plan for a small mosque, Garagus. As in Fathy's other community designs, work, leisure and prayer are closely integrated.

school projects, along with the perceived failure of New Gourna, made him decide to seek more artistic freedom elsewhere.

The general election in 1950 gave the nationalist Wafd party a majority, and rioting in Cairo in January 1952 was an early indication of the dramatic changes that were to follow. The coup of July 1952 left power in the hands of a military regime headed by General Muhammad Nagib. Colonel Gamal Abd al-Nasser, who masterminded the coup, was elected president in June 1956. Fathy must have known that, as a royalist and with close social connections with the court of the overthrown King Farouk, he was in danger.

Crucial to Nasser's plans for modernizing Egypt was the construction of the Aswan High Dam across the Nile – a project that Fathy bitterly criticized throughout his career. In July 1956, the US Secretary of State, John Foster Dulles, displeased by Nasser's warm relations with Soviet bloc countries, withdrew promises of aid to build the dam. Nasser's nationalization of the British- and French-held Suez Canal to raise funds to build the dam, which precipitated the Suez Crisis of 1956, became a symbolic triumph over the West. The Anglo-French and Israeli invasion of Egypt in October 1956 was condemned by the United States and the United Nations, and raised Nasser's prestige within Egypt and the Arab world.

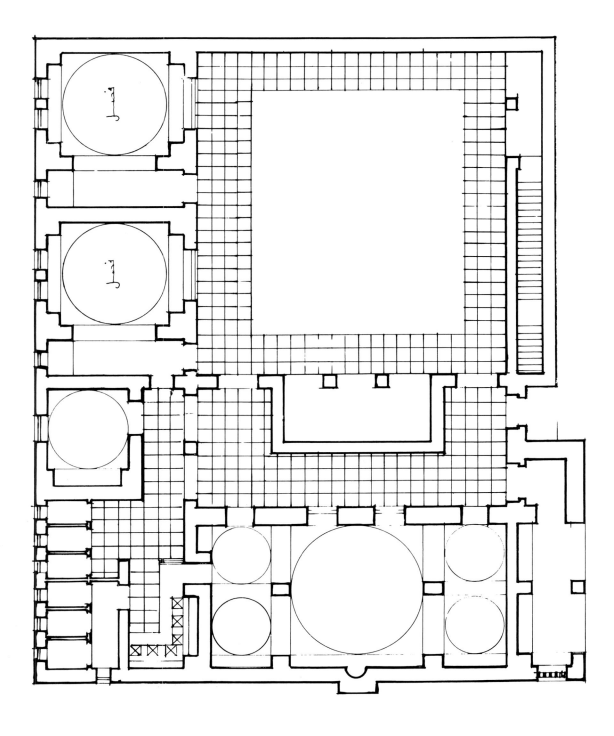

Above The interior of the dome, in the mosque at Lulu'at al-Sahara. In this small agricultural community, the mosque is still meticulously cared for, despite the deterioration of surrounding houses.

Opposite The prayer space, mosque at Lulu'at al-Sahara.

The Monastirli house, 1950. Less vernacular and more ornate than Fathy's other designs of the time, it was conceived after the model of waterside houses along the Bosphorus, Istanbul, in accordance with the client's wishes.

Right Elements of Egyptian Ottoman design may be seen in details such as ornate stained glass windows between conventional fenestration.

Opposite Plan of the Monastirli house. The building is oriented to take best advantage of the river breezes. The formal entry into the house leads from the front door (left of centre in the plan) into a domed central hall. A stairway (shown just below the dome) leads up to an open wooden cupola above a marble fountain overlooking the Nile.

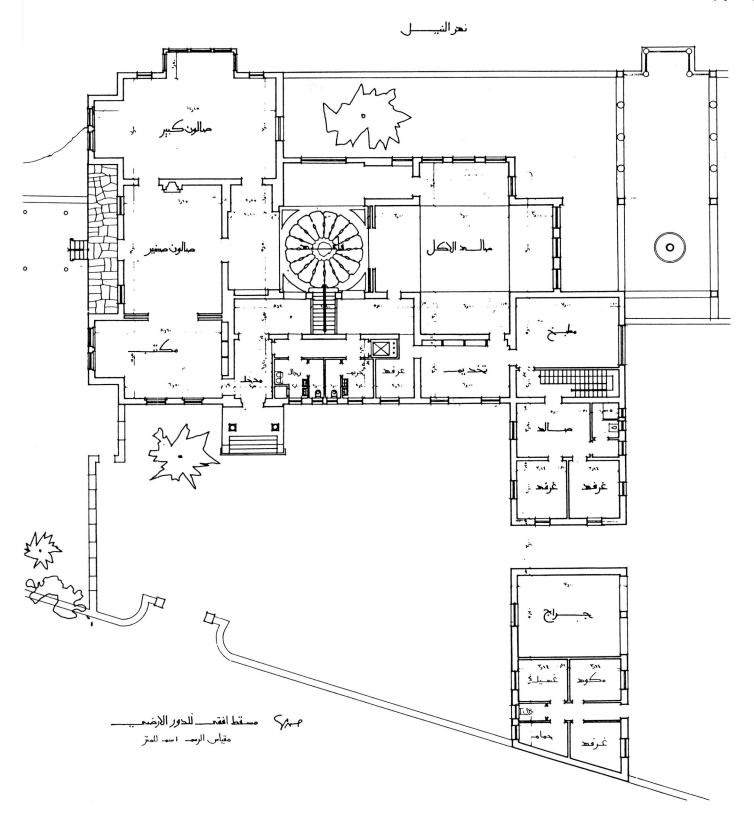

نهر النيـــل

صالون كبير

صالون صغير

مكتب

صالة الاكل

مطبخ

تخديم

غرفة

رجال

محل

صالة

غرفة

غرفة

غرفة

جـراج

غسيلة مكوى

حمام

غرفة

مسقط افقى للدور الارضى
مقياس الرسم ١سم للمتر

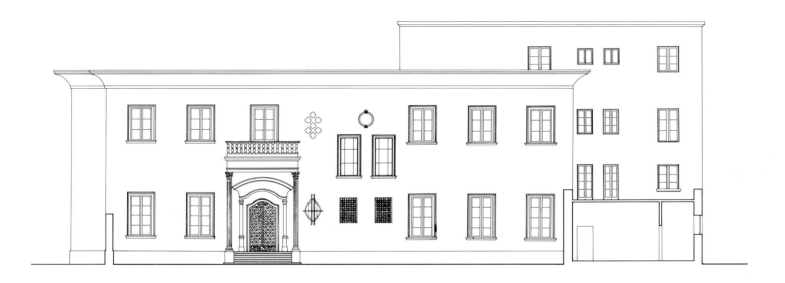

The Monastirli house, 1950. The formal, solid roadside elevation (**above**) gives no hint of the interior courtyard and open riverside outdoor 'room' on the roof on the other side.

Opposite The open wooden pergola on the roof, shaped like a huge lantern, recalls Egyptian Ottoman architecture. The fountain beneath it is situated at the apex of the ornate dome of the formal entrance hall (see elevation, **below**). The window area has been maximized to exploit the cooling effect of river breezes.

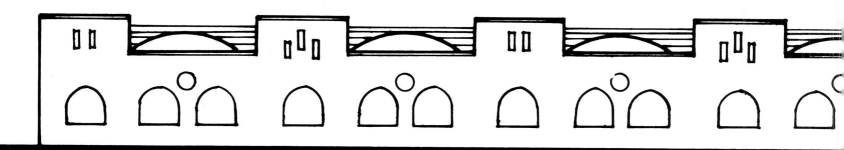

The school at Fares. Fathy designed the building when he was made director of the school building department in 1951 by the Egyptian Ministry of Education.

Below The school combines functional form with environmental sensitivity. Each classroom is served by a wind catch and dome to improve air circulation. The repetitive design of vault and dome over the classrooms (from the left of the elevation) creates a linear counterpoint to the larger domes which rise above the administrative and assembly spaces on the right.

Right The use of natural ventilation in the assembly hall, as throughout the school, provides an inexpensive natural alternative to mechanized forms of air conditioning.

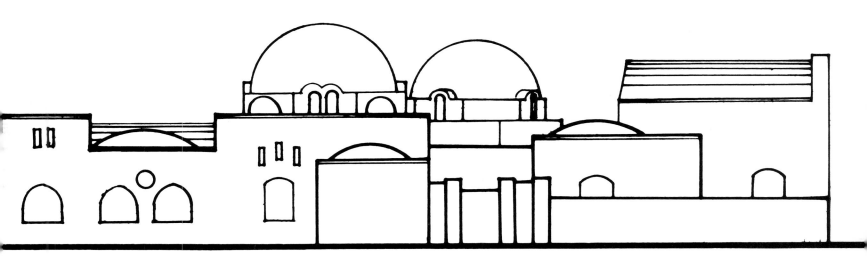

Above and opposite The school at Fares. The massive dome of the administrative centre of the school contrasts with the more intimate scale of the classrooms.

Right The school at Fares. The classrooms were originally to benefit from water pools to aid the cooling of the domed and vaulted space, but due to subsequent alterations they were not used. Despite this, the continuing effectiveness of the natural methods of ventilation testify to the integrity of Fathy's design.

The school at Fares, showing the wind catches above each classroom. Carefully maintained and well served by the community of the secluded island on which it stands, the school continues to thrive. Fathy's design for the schools at Fares and Idfu mark the end of this phase of his career.

Fathy left Egypt in 1956, taking a position with Doxiades Associates, an architectural firm in Athens, where he would stay for five years. It is perhaps ironic that the man who is identified as the champion of an indigenous Egyptian architecture left his homeland at the historic moment that has come to symbolize the end of imperial power in Egypt and the long awaited dawn of its nationalist identity.

At the end of *Architecture for the Poor*, Fathy intimates that misrepresentations of the cost of the school at Fares by government officials in Egypt were his reason for going into voluntary exile. His departure from Cairo was motivated just as much by politics as conscience, in spite of the fact that he would have preferred to convey the impression that it had solely been a matter of principle.

The five years that he spent in Athens, which constitute a critical, and hitherto unexplained chapter in his personal and professional development, also correspond with the formation of the Athens Technological Organization in 1959. Constantinos A. Doxiades, the driving force behind both this and the Athens Centre of Ekistics which followed in 1963, was a visionary architect who had held the position of Chief Town Planning Officer for the Greater Athens Area during the Second World War, while also serving as a corporal in the Greek Army. During the occupation he was Chief of the National Resistance Group, 'Hephaestus', and under difficult circumstances managed to publish a magazine entitled *Regional Planning, Town Planning and Ekistics* prior to the end of the war. As Under-Secretary and Director General of the Ministry of Housing and Reconstruction from 1945 to 1948, and Minister-Coordinator of the Greek

Recovery Programme from 1948 to 1951, Doxiades became deeply involved in problems related to human settlements, within a historical framework, and his position as head of the Greek delegation to the United Nations International Conference on Housing, Planning and Reconstruction in 1947 provided him with his first global exposure to these issues. In 1951 he founded Doxiades Associates with a small group of architects whom he had assembled to work with him on the Recovery Programme, and within twelve years the firm had grown large enough to support projects in forty countries, acquiring its present legal form as DA International Co., Ltd, Consultants on Development and Ekistics, in 1963.

The concept of 'ekistics', which Doxiades first expressed while involved with 'Hephaestus' and which pervades Fathy's writings, has been described by its originator as 'the science of human settlements', conditioned by human parameters and 'influenced by economic, social, political, administrative and technical sciences as well as the disciplines related to the arts'.[1] Derived from the Greek word *oikistikos* ('relating to settlement'), ekistics differs from architecture, in Doxiades's view, in that it goes beyond the specific concerns of one building to incorporate all aspects of the human condition. His exposure to traditional villages in the reconstruction programme after the war led him to believe, like Fathy, that the construction of settlements should involve the entire community, which bonded them in a common belief:

If houses can be built by the people, they should be built by the people. Architecture should not be the private art of a coterie of architects, it should

Left Constantinos Doxiades, founder of Doxiades Associates and the intellectual force behind the Athens Centre for Ekistics (ekistics: the science of human settlements), which Fathy joined in 1956.

Below Meeting of the team behind the City of the Future project. Fathy is visible in profile at the far left; on his left (speaking, with hand raised) is Jacqueline Tyrwhitt. Doxiades is seated at the far right.

be the art of the people, their own expression of their own way of life. But there is one thing which only the government can do: this is to make a plan and a general programme of development for all.[2]

Soon after his arrival in Athens, Fathy took up residence in a small traditional courtyard house on Lycabettus hill at 2 Leukianou Street near the Doxiades office, since removed in the reconstruction of this entire neighbourhood. It is fondly remembered by colleagues of that time as being typical of houses built during the nineteenth century in Athens, a single-storey whitewashed residence with ornate ironwork grilles on the windows, and a pitched red-tiled roof. Rather than being in the middle of the square plan, the courtyard was attached to the entrance, and matched the house in terms of size. Those who visited Fathy remember walking up a short flight of steps to a wooden door on strap hinges set in a high wall covered with hibiscus, and then passing through a courtyard to the entrance of the house itself, which had rooms in enfilade, with very little circulation space inside.

Fathy was initially assigned to the New Cities project in Iraq, which began in 1956 and lasted until 1958. As one of the first major commissions received in the Athens office, the Iraq Housing Programme was significant for Doxiades Associates, providing the opportunity to test theories on a large scale, as well as the economic means to expand operations. Internal memos, circulated among select members of Doxiades Associates in its first office at 10 Venizelou Street, indicate that Fathy was initially involved in the design of the Regional Plan for the Development of Greater Mussayib. He produced both lengthy, researched commentaries on the preliminary plans to be used by the team assigned to this project, and specific designs for what was intended to be a rural farming village. The crux of one commentary from 1958 is that a greater variety of occupations was necessary in the planning of this new settlement in order to ensure its viability and longevity, since purely agricultural villages throughout the Middle East had typically been subject to urban migration, losing many young people to nearby cities, resulting in the virtual extinction of the community.

Using statistics from Europe and America, as well as Gaza, Jordan, and Iraq, Fathy effectively makes the point that well established communities contain a fairly predictable proportion of different trades and that any new settlement, expecting to replicate such stability successfully, should do the same. A portion of his report, related to the 'Classification of Occupations in Gaza', was carried out while he was involved in the design of refugee settlements there as part of a United Nations team during the time he worked for Doxiades. In keeping with the desire for diversity expressed in his report, Fathy's plan for Mussayib reflects his ideas for spatial hierarchy, carried out in the built portion of New Gourna ten years earlier.

Beginning with a central, public area, which includes a *gama'a* (congregational mosque) as well as a *hammam* (public bath), the spaces allocated to the mixed uses preferred by the architect diminish in size until they reach the farmers homes, on the periphery of the village, adjacent to the open fields.[3] Except for the fact that a dimensional grid is used, the planning of Mussayib, and the way that the farmers' homes are organized to have access to open fields in either

Plan of the Ramsis Wissa Wassif Centre, Harraniya. Fathy proposed an extension to the original village in 1957–58, bringing the weavers' houses and workshops close to the plots where the plants for dyes were to be grown.

direction, is particularly reminiscent of his proposals for the Ramsis Wissa Wassif Centre in Harraniya, designed at exactly the same time. Between 1957 and 1958, Fathy proposed an extension to the weaving village that Wissa Wassif had already established on the outskirts of Cairo in 1941. The proposal was clearly organized into studio, sales and residential areas. As in Mussayib, Fathy paid specific attention to the linear arrangement of residential units for the weavers, which are also located on the outer edge of the master plan, and organized in pairs on both sides of the central pedestrian street that runs as a protected means of access between them. They also front directly on fields on either side of each pair, which at Harraniya were intended to grow the plants needed for the natural dyes used by the weavers as well as the food that was meant to make this entire community self-sufficient. This plan utilizes a concept first introduced in Lulu'at al-Sahara, and subsequently extended in New Gourna, in which a rural tradition of protecting valuable livestock inside the house is formalized and livestock access is restricted to the side facing the fields, with the more formal reception areas located near the pedestrian street. In contrast to the uniform, modular rows of Mussayib, the houses in Harraniya are fairly random, with irregular walkways providing visual variety as well as shaded corners in which to sit.[4]

The conceptual, if not formal, similarities between the Harraniya and Mussayib plans, as well as their chronological coincidence, indicate that Fathy returned to Egypt several times during the five-year period in which he was associated with the Doxiades office. Other projects intended for clients in Cairo, with dates that also correspond to this period, such as the

Touheimi Stables and Maaruf Muhammad Maaruf Housing project (1960), the Baume-Marpent Factory in Kharga Oasis (1959), flats for his brother Ali (1960) and Shahira Mehrez (finally completed in 1967), and the Institute of Folk Art, meant to be located in Luxor (1962), all indicate that after an initial period of concern, he felt confident enough to return to Egypt with increasing frequency, until he left Athens in 1962.

A memo from Constantinos Doxiades to Fathy, dated June 21, 1958, regarding the plans for Mussayib, also suggests that the final plans, now preserved in the architect's archive in Cairo, and by the Aga Khan Award in Geneva, represent a revision to an earlier, more individualized scheme similar to those of Lulu'at al-Sahara, New Gourna and Harraniya, using non-orthogonal planning techniques meant to approximate traditional, incremental forms. Given the effect that this memo was to have on the work that was to follow, it deserves to be reproduced here in its entirety:

1.   During the last ten days I have been studying the plans of villages, houses and buildings prepared by Professor Fathy. They are certainly a very important contribution to the research and design work which we are doing. In a few words I would like to say that while our work begins from the national conception and goes down to the details, Professor Fathy has worked from the very smallest detail upwards, building his village.
2.   It is now our duty to combine the two views in order to achieve a really national conception in the spirit of Ekistics which alone can serve the people. The reasons are that generalizations, general systems of ideas etc., can easily overlook

Elevation and plans, Iraq Housing Programme. The repetitive modular units, concrete frame and the International Style elevation are quite uncharacteristic of Fathy's usual vernacular approach (note also the Corbusier-style figures in the drawings of sleeping areas, centre right).

the indispensable details of a master's work, whilst on the other hand, the work only from the details up leads to the danger of not having the possibility of seeing solutions implemented at a scale which is the goal we all share.

3. My remarks on the work already done can be classified in three basic categories: the first category refers to modules – there is an imperative necessity to keep the system of module as we have worked it out up to now for reasons that are well known. I can see that some of the designs of buildings cannot be solved with the Grid system of 3 metres. I propose to use the 3.60 modules system which, implemented on one of the plans of Professor Fathy, has been proved practical.

4. The second basic remark is that we should not design one village or two villages or three villages and their corresponding buildings, houses and facilities but types of villages which can be repeated many times. This should not lead though to the idea to have the same type of village built exactly in the similar way everywhere, as that would be wrong. The unit should be the house and the single building. We therefore need to split the systems of buildings designed by Professor Fathy into types of buildings, one for classes another one for markets, another one for hammams, another one for mosques etc., which can be combined in many different ways. If we keep the grid which we agreed on in the beginning then we can have, in an easier way, several combinations.

5. I therefore beg Professor Fathy to look into

the types of buildings from this angle. We will not certainly have one type of mosque, we will have several and sometimes we cannot design the auxiliary buildings of the mosque which should be the connecting elements between several buildings and the mosque, but we should have the basic part of the mosque designed as a type of mosque. I beg Professor Fathy to look into the work for standardization of buildings which we have been doing lately with 0-GAB [in Iraq].

6. The third type of remark is what I would call a side planning remark since it refers to the movement of pedestrians which should be free from the movement of cars, and to plantation which should be natural, giving three solutions for covered walkways, for green squares, etc. From now on we will proceed in a way to implement these ideas, and give an assistant to Professor Fathy to help him, especially when he will be abroad, in order to reach solutions which are now straightforward because the basic elements have been studied and are the right ones.[5]

A design of a high-rise housing block, intended for the Iraq Housing Programme in general, is totally out of character for Fathy, with its repetitive, box-like units, concrete frame, and International Style elevation. Even the plan drawings, which show figures lying on beds, are reminiscent of a similar convention used by Le Corbusier in his Venice Hospital project, which was highly publicized at this time; and are not typical of Fathy's drawing style. According to Myrto Antonopoulou-Bogdanou, who was involved in this project, several of these units were actually built in

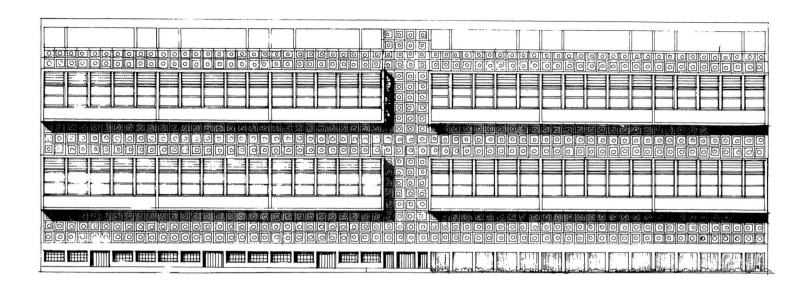

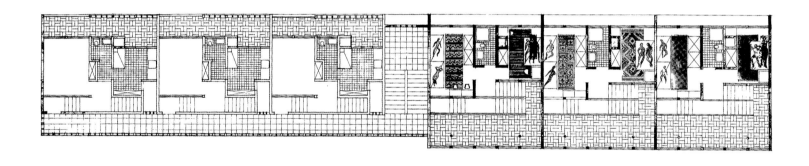

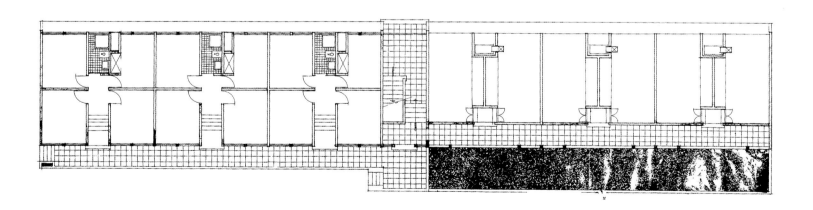

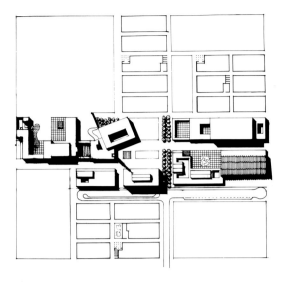

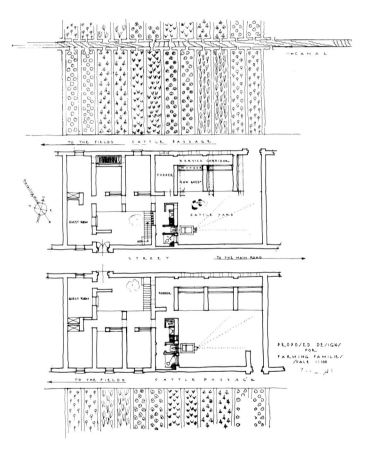

Site plan (**top**) and unit plans, Iraq Housing Programme. In spite of its variance from his earlier projects, this scheme allows for direct access of the inhabitants to their agricultural plots, a characteristic of the Iraqi villages Fathy visited.

Sulimania and Mosul, but they were so unpopular that armed guards were needed to keep people in them prior to the Revolution in 1959. Afterwards they were abandoned, and their occupants went back to the *sarifas*, or mud houses, they had come from. Such an aberration in the career of the same architect who was able to conceptualize and partially realize the village of New Gourna against all odds only ten years earlier, is startling, to say the least. It is more understandable, perhaps, when considered within the context of the Mussayib memo from Doxiades, issued several months earlier, which strongly suggests a more rationalistic approach, as well as the need for 'standardization', and an assistant to help him 'reach solutions' based on 'basic elements', while he is abroad on his many travels. One might also consider Fathy's concern for personal safety, adaptation to new, and more liberal surroundings and the requirement of having to work with a team after having been accustomed to almost complete autonomy for more than twenty-five years of practice. The Iraqi high-rises contravene all of Fathy's principles, and yet do show an attempt, within extremely stringent parameters, to mitigate an unremitting typology with innovative ideas for cross-ventilation and layers of privacy, without doors. Taken as a whole, the Housing Programme and Mussayib projects, when considered against the scheme of both earlier and later work, as well as the compelling atmosphere that prevailed in Athens at this time, represent an important turning point in Fathy's career, since he can be seen to have retained many of the useful ideas he was exposed to there. These include the efficiency of the module in the design of prototypical buildings, and the concept of universality which is integral to ekistics.

One of the trips 'abroad' that Doxiades was referring to in his memo to Fathy was a mission to Syria, which was part of the United Arab Republic at that time, and therefore under the control of General Abd al-Nasser, in order to assist Panagis Psomopoulos in negotiations related to projects in Homs, Hama and Selemiyah. In his recollections of that trip, which took place in the latter part of 1959, and lasted almost two weeks, Psomopoulos has related that the head of the planning department in Syria was an Egyptian, as well as a former student of Fathy, and that Doxiades personally proposed that Fathy be included in the delegation in order to ensure the success of the presentation. Rather than being helpful, however, he also recalls that Fathy was particularly irascible and interfering during questioning about specific aspects of the Master Plan, to the extent that Psomopoulos became concerned that his presence may have jeopardized its acceptance.

Following his involvement in the Iraqi Housing Programme, and Planning for Mussayib Village, and after a brief connection with both the Human Community in Athens project, Fathy was connected with the establishment of the curriculum for a post-graduate School of Ekistics. This initially included thirty Pakistani students from Islamabad, who arrived in Athens in early 1960.

Soon afterwards, Fathy was assigned to the City of the Future project, which was housed in new offices at 26 Fokylidou Street in order to give it autonomy. Funded by the 25 per cent of income derived from architectural and planning projects that Doxiades allocated for research, as well as from additional sources, the City of the Future project represented an audacious attempt at developing forecasting analogies that would facilitate the prediction of change in human settlements. Intended to be a long-term forecasting project on a scale previously unattempted, the purpose of the initiative was to go beyond architecture, and the physical form of cities into systems, structures and networks, using methods derived from biological, physiological, ecological and anthropological sciences to predict growth.[6] As described by John Papaioannou, who collaborated with Doxiades in producing the published results of the project in 1974:

> The concept of the City of the Future was born in the Athens Centre of Ekistics in the year 1960. By the end of the 1950s we could not see any progress being made anywhere in the world in attempts to deal with the urgent problems of our cities. People did not even seem to be concerned, at that time, when we tried to draw attention to the urban crisis; we were accused of frightening people. We therefore asked ourselves: what is going to happen? Are we going to go on living in the cities of the present which get increasingly worse with every day that passes because of their continuous growth, or are we going to live in these utopian cities which so many people talk about, but which never actually get built because they cannot [be] and because many even should not be built? We did not know the answer, so we decided to become more serious about it and begin a research project to find out.[7]

The project began with a core of participants including Myrto Antonopoulou-Bogdanou, who became its Project Manager in 1965, Dr R. I. Meier,

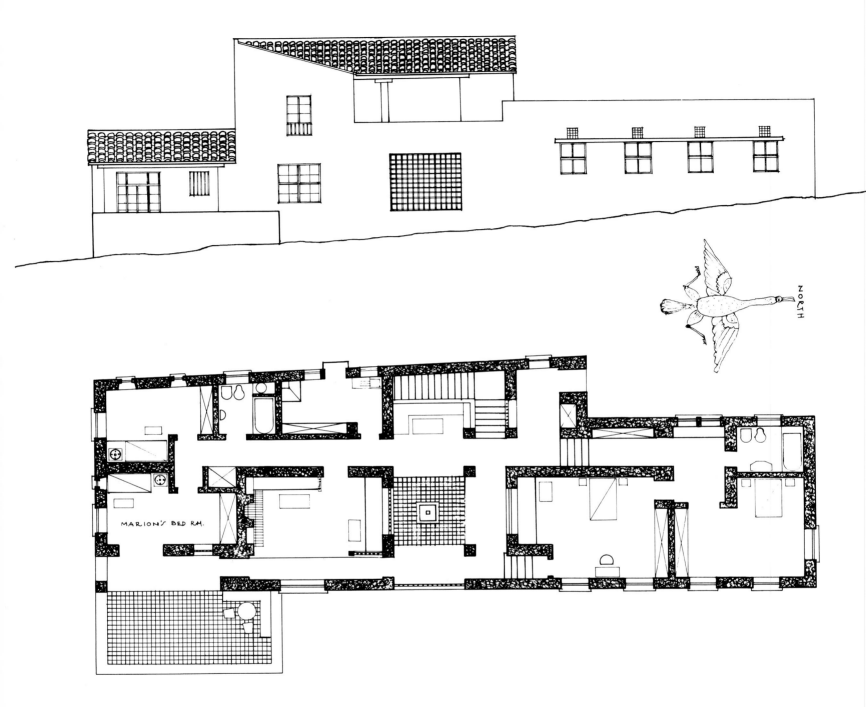

MARION'S BED RM.

Elevation and plan of Carr house. Marion Carr, a colleague of Fathy's on the City of the Future team, wanted to take advantage of the view from the site at Liodessi, outside Athens; Fathy's design sought privacy. This subtle difference of cultures meant that Fathy failed to win the commission.

Professor Jacqueline Tyrwhitt, Professor J. Matos Mar, Professor M. Gomez Mayorga, and Professor G. Gutenschwager. Over the next fourteen years, it expanded to include nearly 150 participants at various levels, including John Searles, Auguste Arsac, Panagis Psomopoulos, Dimitrios Iatrides, Brian Berry, Catherine Hughes-Nagashima, Marion Carr, Georges Papageorgious, Jean Gottman and Arnold Toynbee.

While his contacts in Athens were not limited to these professional associations, and especially extended to what Panagis Psomopoulos has described as the 'musical milieu' of the city, towards which he gravitated because of his own love for the violin, Fathy did establish friendships with several of the people with whom he worked at 26 Fokylidou Street.

The composer Iannis Xenakis, who was living and working in Paris at this time, studied engineering at the Athens Polytechnic, and served as Secretary to the Resistance after the invasion of Greece. Xenakis worked with Le Corbusier, and his influence, together with that of Doxiades, may explain Fathy's apparent drift into the Modernist camp with the Iraq project.

The degree to which the abstractions taking place in architecture during the late 1950s and early 1960s had an equivalent in music is striking, as is the fact that Fathy was undoubtedly experiencing an equal amount of intellectual struggle in each of the areas of his artistic life that mattered to him most. Many prominent figures around him professed popular sympathies and social and historical awareness, but produced architecture and music that irrevocably broke with past traditions.

John Papaioannou has provided an intriguing insight into the kind of reciprocal influence that may have been generated by such social connections in his vivid recollections of a specific dinner party, hosted by Fathy in the open courtyard of his house, soon after the City of the Future project began. Papaioannou recalls that as well as himself, guests included the historian Arnold Toynbee and his wife, the Mexican professor Gomez Mayorga, and the composer Iannis Christo. After dinner, Christo, who had an extensive understanding of oriental religions as well as mysticism and the occult, initiated a discussion about the values of tradition in society, which quickly turned into a polarized debate. Papaioannou remembers that Professor Mayorga promoted the Modernist view, and that Fathy and Christo both opposed him, with Arnold Toynbee remaining neutral. Papaioannou especially remembers this particular exchange above all others because of the brilliance of the arguments on both sides and the unchallenged claims of victory by the traditionalists at the conclusion of the debate.

This was a rare and exhilarating time for all of those associated with Doxiades. Architect-philosopher R. Buckminster Fuller, although not directly associated with the City of the Future project, did participate in conferences and symposia, and judging solely from Fathy's adoption of the geodesic dome as a roof form in several of the buildings he designed in the middle and late 1960s, Fuller was an important influence on his attitude toward technology.

Marion Carr, who was connected with the City of the Future team, was another associate, who provided the single known opportunity for Fathy to design and build in Greece during his stay there. Because of her academic background in social anthropology, she was responsive to the concept of ekistics, and gradually became involved with the organization. She eventually bought a piece of land from Jacqueline Tyrwhitt in Liodessi, outside Athens, in the hope of building a traditional Greek house, and asked Fathy to design a modest, inexpensive residence for her. He consequently produced two designs which each took advantage of a north–south ridge running through the site, and a beautiful view to the east. In Carr's opinion, however, neither proposal was satisfactory, having too little fenestration on the eastern elevation, making it difficult to appreciate the visual quality the location had to offer. Perhaps out of reticence to confront the architect with what was obviously a cultural issue related to privacy, Carr sold the land back to the original owner and bought an existing house on the island of Serifos instead. She eventually diverted her passion for traditional Athenian architecture, which Fathy's designs capture with their whitewashed walls and pitched red-tiled roofs, into an extensive report on more than 2000 examples of nineteenth-century houses in that city.

No records have yet been found of Fathy's travels around Greece, but mention of certain areas both in this report and in his later writings, particularly regarding details of certain designs, indicate they were extensive. Mentioned are the monastery on Mount Athos, the islands of Chios, Mykonos and Santorini in the Cyclades, and the Hellenistic city of Priene in Asia Minor, confirming his curiosity about a culture which had so much in common with his own. There is an identifiable relationship between his later work and Cycladic forms which have evolved in direct response to social, environmental and material variants similar to those that had informed his own architecture.[8]

In the autumn of 1960, Fathy was asked to visit various parts of Africa in conjunction with an effort to compile reports on global regions for study by the City of the Future group; and he submitted a preliminary itinerary soon afterward that included eighteen cities in North, West and Central Africa.[9] He timed the beginning of his trip to correspond with a seminar in Cairo organized around the theme of 'The New Metropolis in the Arab World,' which took place from 17 to 22 December, 1960, in which he presented a paper entitled 'Planning and Building in the Arab Tradition: The Village Experiment at Gourna'. As subsequently edited by Monroe Berger, and published in the following year, this paper provides an interesting insight into Fathy's state of mind after three years with Doxiades. He speculated on the ways in which the historical 'trinity' of architect, craftsman, and client might be re-established, in order to arrest the decline of popular culture that he perceived as the root cause of the disintegration of the quality of urban life.

Fathy also addressed the idea of 'sectors' promoted by Doxiades, to which he also frequently refers in his report on cities in Africa, and which, in retrospect, corresponds at a larger scale to the *badanas* or neighbourhoods he initiated in New Gourna. Each sector is intended to be a self-sufficient community in its own right, with services, such as schools and shops, located within it, as they would be in a small town, to make it physically and psychologically comprehensible to the inhabitants. The final message of the paper is his strong belief that ekistic principles, and sectoring, as proposed by Doxiades, combined with a recognition of the historical formulation of architectural space, and the re-involvement of the client in the building process, are the only possible ways of reversing current trends, to create 'a truly great Arab Metropolis in the future'.[10]

Fathy did not view his association with Doxiades as simply a collaboration of convenience, but was anxious to promote the basic tenets of ekistics to an audience who knew him well, tempering it with an appeal for a return to traditional values. His theoretical position was precariously balanced between a belief in the inevitability of change, on the one hand, and an equally strong conviction that such change should come about within a regional framework, on the other. This theme was novel at the time, but has now become conventional wisdom. External governments and institutions who genuinely want to help Africa, in which the local share of the world's gross national product has dropped from 1.9 per cent to 1.2 per cent in the thirty-one years since Fathy wrote his reports, now echo his sentiments. As one journal has recently reported, it is beginning to be acknowledged that

> Africa has its own 'centres', its resources of vitality and resilience. It operates by its own inner dynamics and metaphysics. Africa looks hopeless, but it is not. In many ways the continent is headed in the right direction for the first time in centuries. Real changes for the better are occurring. Africa is evolving African solutions.[11]

Fathy's reports on his visits to African cities make up a significant part of his contribution to the City of the Future effort, with the other part concentrating on general considerations of time, contemporaneity, religion, aesthetics and planning techniques. Purposely steering clear of a statistical basis for comparison, since the difficulty of obtaining such information at that time would have been impractical, he intuitively argues for

a more qualitative approach in any subsequent studies which may be made in future, noting that Africa resists 'numerical proscription'. While recognizing that common characteristics exist between each of these cities, he intentionally isolates specific, identifiable differences. There is exquisite irony in the fact that Fathy criticizes European intervention in African affairs, which had disastrous consequences since it bled away its most valuable resources at a point in its historical development when they were needed most, since this is a cultural tradition that influenced him greatly. It is always clear, as he says in his conclusion to his report on his visit to the cities of Africa, that his criticisms are severe 'only because I judge Europeans by their own highest standards, and compare what has actually been done with what could have been done. But far worse has been done by Arabs, for example, to their own people.'

A rather strange unsigned document found among his papers, which can only be attributed to Fathy by the secretarial designation 'HF/em' at the bottom of the last page, is dated 19 May 1961, which corresponds with his preparation of the reports on the cities he visited in Africa. Under the heading 'Le Christ Recrucifié', the title of a novel by the Greek writer Nikos Kazantzakis, Fathy simply lists outrageous quotes related to the slave trade in Africa without further commentary.[12] By confining each quote to a single page, the effect of each is intentionally heightened, giving the entire grouping a cinematic, documentary quality that drives its point home quite effectively. In addition to the document's demonstration of Fathy's conviction that European exploitation was responsible for the retarded state of development of the continent,

'Le Christ Recrucifié', along with his general introduction, also provides valuable insights into the character and extent of the reading list that he assembled prior to making the journey to Africa, which included sources as diverse as Teilhad de Chardin and the United States Department of Commerce.

One of the most puzzling of all of the paradoxes surrounding Fathy is that his historicism and the belief in progress that it implied is at odds with the synchronic philosophy he has come to represent. In reality, his activities during the five years he was in Athens indicate that while he continued to look to the past for inspiration, he thrived on the energy of the present, and expectantly anticipated the future, seeing no discrepancy in the facility with which he was able to compartmentalize each. A change to a reliance on orthogonal co-ordinates that began in Greece may be traced through Fathy's work in Egypt from 1962.

In addition to such linearity, there is another change in Fathy's work, following his return from Athens, of a more overtly nationalistic architecture. It is as if, in compensation for his allegiance to international concepts, expressed in ekistics, he felt compelled to align himself more closely with those willing to finance projects that would educate the public about Egyptian history.

While superficially appearing to conform to the ekistic thesis, Fathy's report differs from it in several significant ways, all related to his more humanistic, and less strictly rational world view. Doxiades perceived ekistics as a study involving co-ordination, and reconciliation between economists, sociologists, politicians, and all of the disciplines related to the arts. As a 'science of human settlements', it was not seen by him to be restricted to architecture or urban planning but to involve many different fields of human endeavour. Where Doxiades saw the overwhelming need for unity in his vision of ekistics, however, Fathy saw diversity, and the importance in encouraging local differences, to prevent cultural identity from being eradicated. Doxiades spoke of 'integration', but Fathy characterized the process as one of 'entropy', so that as each city grew, it would retain its own special character, rather than being an unrecognizable global urban zone. With such differentiation in mind, Fathy addressed the issue of time, substituting the concept of 'growth rhythm' for urban expansion in synchronic calendar time, with the implication that each city has singular characteristics and should not be evaluated using uniform criteria. His discussion of contemporaneity, which has such relevance in architecture today when the social, environmental, cultural and financial cost of innovation is coming under increasing scrutiny, is generated from the premise of the relevance of time, and the need for relative standards in measuring it. The sophistication inherent in such a distinction, when compared with the tendency toward historicism mentioned earlier, make it obvious that Fathy cannot be easily categorized.[13]

Fathy's City of the Future report, which was just one of 258 internal reports produced by the project, totalling almost 10,000 pages, with a further 1700 pages of maps, graphs, and drawings, was subsumed into 'the red book', entitled *Ecumenopolis: The Inevitable City of the Future* published under the names of Constantinos Doxiades and John G. Papaioannou, in 1976. It was one of four 'red books' that Doxiades saw as the final documentation and summary of his life's work.

It accompanied *Anthropopolis: City for Human Development* (1975), and *Building Utopia and Action for Human Settlements* (1976). Papaioannou, in his preface to *Ecumenopolis*, freely admits that the book was only intended as a summary, rather than the official report of the City of the Future project, and because of the working formula used to produce it, is 'much more a personal view of its two authors'. He goes on to note, however, that since

> these were continuously and deeply involved in the project, and responsible for it, this attempt at a first comprehensive synthesis purports to sum up the total experience gained through the research project and to present it, for the first time, in as unified a vision as…possible at the present stage of evolution of ideas around the central concept of the City of the Future.

With Doxiades's death in 1975, no official report by the group on the City of the Future was ever begun, leaving *Ecumenopolis* as the sole record and interpretation of the internal reports of which Fathy's findings were a part, and in July 1991, these reports, stored in the Library of the Athens Centre of Ekistics, began to be destroyed.

Subsequent initiatives, such as the Earth Summit in Brazil, have borne out the need for global action on the entire range of issues that Doxiades championed, but in the intervening years, it has become clear that population growth is a far more arcane, and unpredictable factor than the four 'red books' would lead us to believe, not 'inevitably' leading to the worldwide conurbation that he predicted.

For all of their originality and thoughtfulness, Fathy's findings never surface in *Ecumenopolis*, but are transmuted into a single diagram of the nations he visited, purporting to show the form, and phasing of the 'world city' there, as well as its final extent. John Papaioannou has privately characterized Fathy's contribution in his African studies as one of infinite faith in the people themselves, rather than in the opinion of outside 'experts' who secretly regard them as primitive and backward. Fathy's reports recognize that Africans are guided by principles that outsiders cannot understand, and the wisdom of this view has only recently come to be appreciated.

Shortly after Constantinos Doxiades died, Margaret Mead and Buckminster Fuller presented his four 'red books' to the United Nations as a gesture of their global significance, and the City of the Future project came to an end. *Architecture for the Poor*, which had appeared approximately three years before his friends made their presentation to the United Nations, remained the single source for those interested in Fathy's work, and has brought him international recognition and a public following that has continued to identify him with ideals associated with one brief period of a long career. This legacy has obscured other facets of his personality. While he was deeply committed to those whom he called 'the economic untouchables' of the world, and continued to search for solutions to the chronic housing problems faced by the poor, primarily through appropriate technologies, his interests ranged far wider than self-help projects such as New Gourna. The City of the Future offers additional insight into their wider scope, and the intellect of this complex man.

4
Late Career: 1967–89

While working on a large palace at Tabuk in the Kingdom of Saudi Arabia in 1974, Hassan Fathy was commissioned by the United Nations Organization for Rural Development to visit the town of Dariya as an advisor. His specific task was to design a prototypical house that would serve as a model for others like it to be built throughout the country to improve village life. The project provided a way for him to study a culture that had a strong relationship with Egyptian culture and evolved in a distinctive way. This uniqueness is especially evident in the central region of the Najd, where Dariya is located, because of its isolation in the middle of the large expanse of desert that has ensured its security and relative independence from outside influence for centuries. This freedom allowed the region to evolve a distinctive architectural character.

What Fathy found on his arrival at Dariya was a small oasis town, dramatically sited on a high bluff overlooking the lush greenery of the Wadi Hanifa below, which flows through the capital city of Riyadh about fifteen kilometres away, to the northwest.

Opposite Wind catch, New Baris.

Right The distinctive forms of traditional Najd architecture near Riyadh, which inspired Fathy in his new designs for a United Nations pilot project in Dariya, Saudi Arabia.

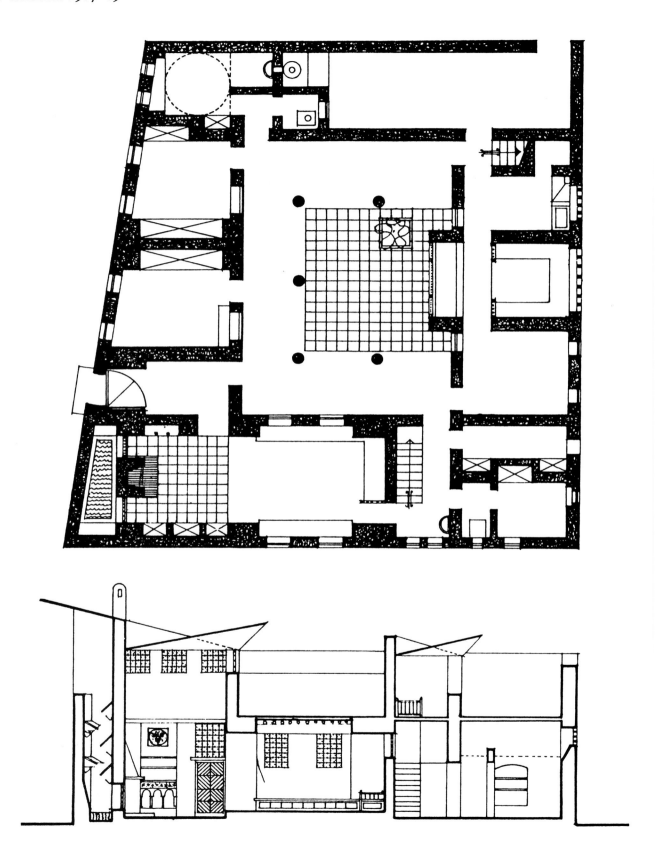

Plan and section of housing prototype for Dariya. Fathy was guided by existing examples in local villages. Note the offset *mojabab* entrance (**above**, left of centre), protecting interior privacy; and the *baratsi* wind catch and baffles (**below**, far left of drawing). The roof terrace (**below**, centre) is often used as a sleeping area.

The village occupied only the south bank of the river, which it had bridged in the past. The entire settlement, including the part on the northern bank which was known as al-Turayf, is thought to have been established as early as the fifteenth century, but really only came to prominence as the centre of a religious reform movement led by the Imam Muhammad Abd al-Wahab who was joined in this effort by the Emir Muhammad Ibn Saud. Because of this initiative, and its strategic defensive position, the town later came under attack from troops sent by Muhammad Ali of Egypt in 1818, and many of the buildings there were badly damaged or destroyed in the fierce fighting and bombardment.

More than two hundred houses that did remain habitable, and the shells of palaces and other public buildings, presented Fathy with the image of an identifiable and distinctive architectural style and construction method. Using local stone as a foundation, stem-walls up to about one metre above the ground line were used to support a mud-brick wall above. These walls are made of a mixture called *allaben*, consisting of either earth or sand mixed with crushed gypsum and straw. The entire wall is then covered with *alyer* or mud plaster to protect it from the surprisingly heavy spring rains that are common to this region.

The six major goals set out by Fathy in his design of the Dariya prototype unit were: (1) the improvement of the standards of sanitation that he found in the village; (2) the preservation of the distinctive architectural style of this area; (3) the use of local building materials; (4) the improvement of construction techniques that had been used in the past; (5) the respect for the traditions and customs of the region; and (6) the provision of means of heating and cooling that would avoid the use of expensive mechanical equipment. Before he began the design, he analysed many of the empty and partially destroyed houses in the village and broke them down into the component spaces that he found typical in each. These he listed as entrance, courtyard, reception room, living room, bedrooms, bath, kitchen and roof, which he also noted has traditionally been used as an outside sleeping area in this country. He found the offset *mojabab* entrances to the houses here to be much like the *magaz* in Cairo, with the front door opening up to a blank wall that screens the interior from outside view and protects the privacy of the family inside. This entrance typically leads into a central courtyard, which acts as a temperature regulator for the rooms surrounding it, allowing them to have windows looking out onto it and in order to present a blank wall to neighbours. Because these courts are usually left unpaved, they are frequently covered with large reed mats that allow it to be used as a sitting area during the cooler parts of the day, which makes it a social space for the entire family and an ideal, protected place for children to play.

Having made the pilgrimage to Mecca for the Haj, Fathy had also been able to visit al-Madina al-Munawrah. He made special note of the traditional houses there, which he found much more refined than those he had seen in Dariya, using a series of open spaces to create convection currents in much the same way as at the Bayt al-Suhaymi and other medieval houses in Cairo. Dr Jamil Akhbar, a Saudi architect, has carried out extensive research on the al-Madina houses and his surveys show a configuration of spaces much

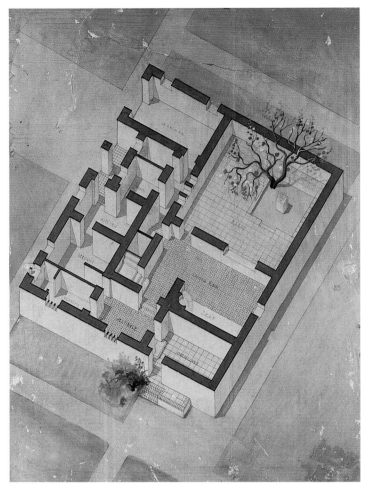

Axonometric plan in gouache. This unidentified project shows how Fathy divided the public and private zones of a house – here by means of a central 'spine' (from above right to below left of the drawing), each side with its own entrance.

Opposite Fathy describes the use of the *baratsi* roof truss at Sohar, Oman. An alternative where mud bricks were not available, the strong, lightweight truss was made from locally obtained split reeds, combined with chickenwire and cement. *Baratsis* were also used extensively at Dariya, Saudi Arabia.

like the Cairene *qa'a*, indicating that its typological evolution may have taken place simultaneously in several locations, or that these houses were influenced by their Egyptian counterparts.

A *majlis*, or reception room for male guests, is also an important part of the traditional house plan in Dariya, just as it is throughout Saudi Arabia. In the Najd, this space is usually accommodated with the *mojabab*, either in a separate room, or in a screened-in part of the courtyard. Since refreshments and meals are usually served to the guests by an unseen hostess who passes the food through a door from the preparation area, it is necessary for the *majlis* to be as close to the kitchen as possible, and also to have direct access to a room for washing the hands after a meal.

Fathy proposed several versions of what he called a 'developed model' of the traditional Dariya house, rigorously subjecting the section of each one to the known sun-path angles for various times of the day and year in this area in order to be sure that shadow was projected onto the open courtyard and the various parts of the house that surrounded it. These diagrams allowed him to raise or lower the massing of the various parts of the house accordingly, as well as to change the orientation, length and width of the courtyard itself. As in each of his projects, his final plan is an ingenious lesson in the separation of public and private areas that is so important in the Islamic world. The inner court of traditional houses of the area is usually at the centre, with all of the other spaces lined up in a square band of uniform width around it; here it defers to the *majlis*, which is recognized as the most problematic space, and therefore the one to be dealt with most directly. Fathy overcomes the seemingly difficult connection between the *majlis* and the kitchen by situating the *majlis* at the centre around which all of the other spaces of the house logically take up their positions. The importance of the *majlis* stems from the Bedouin code of hospitality, which rather than just being a formality in the past, may have meant the difference between survival or death in the desert for those to whom it was offered.

Of the two entrances, the larger, square, recessed entry on the left is reserved for guests. After passing around the *mojabab*, visitors are led to either a more formal sitting area on the left-hand corner of this entry zone, or a dining area in the central core. The entrances are both strategically placed in front of the threshold into the court, which has been recognized as the private domain of the family or very close friends. The typical ritual of hospitality is that introductory formalities would normally take place in the larger room to the left, which would be followed by a meal in the second, more centralized room across the hall, adjoining the kitchen. For this reason, the first, larger *majlis* is more elaborate than the dining area, with low seats facing each other to facilitate extended conversation. For the first time, Fathy introduced a lightweight and highly economical roof truss, called a *baratsi*; this folded slab was an important element of his later design, the development of which he was to describe later:

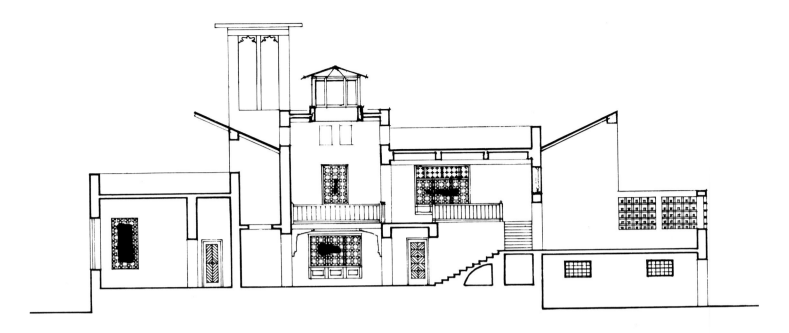

Section of the Nassif house, Jeddah, showing the *qa'a* and *malkaf*. The house bears some of the finest ornamental woodwork to be found in Fathy's buildings.

When I was working in Greece I began to think about what other materials might be available in hot-arid climates where they don't have mud bricks like we do. It was interesting because I like the challenge of change and don't like the repetition of anything in art. They have reeds and other plants, so I thought of using reeds for roofing, giving the resistance of geometric form to the reeds. In using the folded slab, the ratio between the thickness of the slab and the span is 1:2000, so in a room with a 3-metre span the thickness of the slab is something like 4 millimetres. I made a folded slab with reeds normally used for fishing rods, covered them with chickenwire and sprayed them with a thin layer of cement. It took about one ton of loading per square metre without any effect and was naturally ventilated because it was open on one side.[1]

Fathy used this truss most effectively in a reconstruction project in Sohar, in the Sultanate of Oman, to restore a market area destroyed by fire in 1967. The *baratsi* were perfect for this application because they could be prefabricated cheaply, erected quickly, and performed well in the hot, humid climate of the area. A *baratsi* wind catch with an inner *salsabil* (water-cooling plate) is provided in the Dariya model for cool air on warm summer evenings with a fireplace to take the chill off the cold desert nights. A stairway, directly connected to this *majlis*, leads up to the roof, and was intended for use on evenings when even the wind catch was not able to cool the interior. This is due to the thermal lag of earthen walls, which keep the inside of such houses cool during the day, but radiate the heat that they store into the house at night. For this reason many countries throughout the hot-arid and hot-humid regions of the Middle East use the roof as an outdoor 'room' for sitting out and sleeping at night. In giving over a part of this 'room' to guests, Fathy recognized their equal need for comfort, and he incorporated a very high parapet wall running between the guest and family areas there, to retain the privacy of each, making unintentional contact between family and guests highly unlikely. The intricate crenellations shown on the roof parapet in the elevation are an elaborate version of a similar detail traditionally used on roofs throughout the village, and also indicates the higher status given to the roof by this additional use. The distinctive decoration of the crenellations, characteristic of the Najd in general and of Dariya in particular, is recalled in the highly ornamental door for family use on the right-hand side of the main facade, which leads into the kitchen, living, dining and bedroom zone of the house, and has access to a bathroom of its own.

A second stair, diametrically opposite to the one intended for guests, also leads up to the roof from this quarter, emphasizing the existence of two zones above.

One of these prototypes was actually built, in much modified form, and its environmental performance has reportedly been very good. Although never implemented on a large scale, this project, and the United Nations' interest in this community, heightened national awareness of its importance, and ultimately led to its restoration, along the lines recommended by Fathy, as befitting a village with such an illustrious history and memorable architectural style.

In an award-winning study for the new town of Yanbu on the Red Sea coast of Saudi Arabia by the American firm of Skidmore, Owings and Merrill in 1975, a list of proposed passive cooling strategies was heralded in the western press as revolutionary in its proposals for energy-conscious design for the hot-arid regions of the Middle East. Each of the strategies that were listed, such as the use of thermal mass, shading, careful fenestration patterns for cross-ventilation, materials chosen for reflectance value, and diurnal and seasonal zoning of spaces in the design process, had all been intentionally integrated in this Dariya prototype. Fathy's work anticipated all of the studies that followed, but was accompanied by far less fanfare.

The Abd al-Rahman Nassif villa in Jeddah represents another important attempt by Fathy to reinterpret the traditional architecture of Saudi Arabia, in this case on a palatial scale. It was one of the first new villas in Jeddah to recall traditional forms and spatial arrangements. The Nassif house, built out of local coral rock partially retrieved from buildings being demolished in the old quarter of the city, is also one of the finest examples of Fathy's use of ornamental woodwork.

The two decades following Fathy's return to Egypt were the most productive of his career, with two significant projects bringing the issues he formulated at New Gourna full circle. The first was at New Baris in the Kharga Oasis. The discovery of an enormous water source in the central desert of Egypt in 1963, an ancient artesian well near Kharga with a capacity estimated to be sufficient to irrigate 1000 acres, led the Desert Development Organization to commission a design for an agricultural community, initially to house 250 families. His previous experience with such a project, and his ability to build it inexpensively, made Fathy the logical choice as the architect of New Baris. Unlike New Gourna, however, the inhabitants of this proposed agricultural community were not known, and so he concentrated on a more prototypical approach. With the Aswan High Dam having prevented the annual flooding of the Nile and the subsequent fresh coating of rich black silt that the river deposited on the fields bordering its banks, the Egyptian government issued an edict to prohibit the stripping of the only remaining topsoil, bringing to an end the centuries-old practice of mud-brick making. Due to its interior location, Baris was not affected by this ban, but Fathy decided that he would try to use this opportunity to develop a new technique for making sand brick, which might also give Egypt a new industry.

This page and opposite The village of Old Kharga in Egypt's central desert is built from mud brick. Fathy was inspired by traditional methods of escaping the oppressive desert heat: many of the streets (**opposite and below**) are covered to provide protection from the sun; houses are built around courtyards in close configurations to create shade.

With this material in mind, and realizing that no surveys or plans of local villages were available to him, he used the traditional village typology itself, with its winding streets and introverted forms, as a guide, with the reassurance that in villages like Old Kharga nearby, these tactics worked to offset the harsh climate. The existing village of Baris is brick, with compact forms and party walls, grouped around covered streets in a configuration that is similar to those found in archaeological digs throughout the region. In this forbidding desert, where summer temperatures can exceed 50 degrees centigrade, such timeless strategies have been the only way to survive.

Plan of New Baris, in the Kharga Oasis in the central desert. The market is shown centre left; the mosque, offset with a central courtyard, is centre right.

Opposite An interior passage in the market at New Baris, one of the few buildings to be completed before war stopped construction of the new community in 1967.

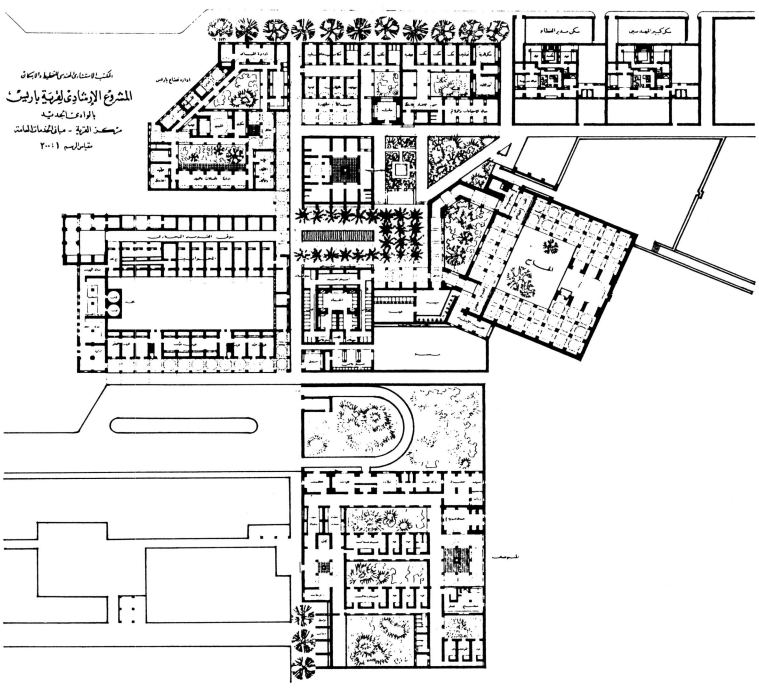

Desert temperatures at New Baris, intended as an agricultural settlement, posed a challenge: how to store fresh produce which was liable to perish quickly. By building the storage area of the market below grade, and with the sophisticated use of natural methods of ventilation, Fathy was able to achieve temperature reductions by as much as 15 degrees centigrade.

Opposite and below Ascending ranks of wind catches on the roof of the market faced the prevailing desert breeze.

Left Vaulted mud-brick construction ensured good air circulation and efficient insulation from heat.

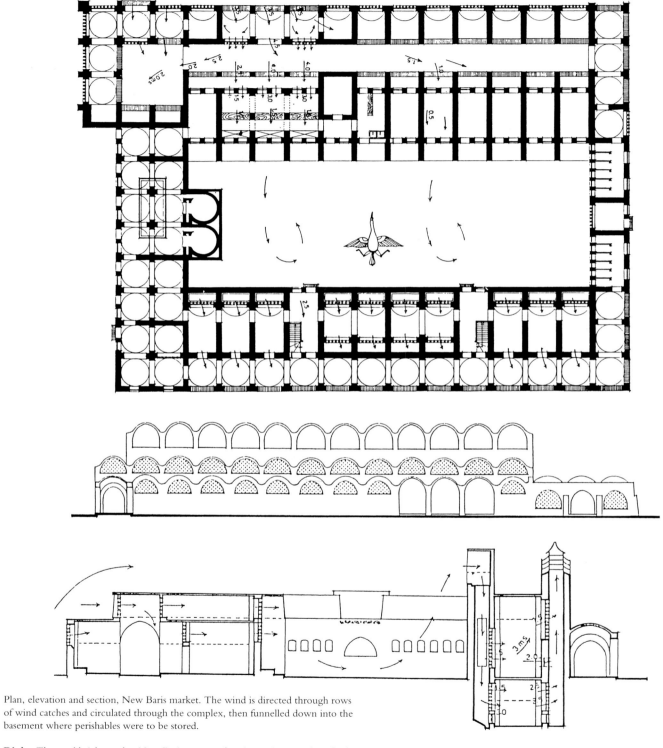

Plan, elevation and section, New Baris market. The wind is directed through rows of wind catches and circulated through the complex, then funnelled down into the basement where perishables were to be stored.

Right The mud bricks used at New Baris were made using an improved method over those used in Old Kharga. Fathy, distrustful of many who used his ideas without giving due credit, did not write down the formula; it has now been lost.

Below Market, New Baris. Deep-set arches and vaults constructed with openwork screens serve both practical and decorative functions.

Opposite View from inside a *malkaf* (wind catch).

Beginning with the image of the Tunisian desert village, and considering the observations he had made in Fatimid Cairo, Fathy laid out the main streets of the plan in a north–south direction so that they would remain in shade most of the day, deviating from this principle only when necessary to conform to changes in topography. The village centre was at the heart of his concept, consisting of a large mosque, a hospital, administration offices, a *suq* and a 'Moorish Café'. There are no vast open squares baking in the sun, but interior courtyards within each building as in Arab villages in the past.

As the activity centre of this agricultural enterprise, the *suq* is one of the most important buildings and it became the ultimate test of Fathy's attempt to ameliorate the extremely harsh conditions without mechanical means. The *suq* not only had to function efficiently as a place to work and shop, but as a cool storage area for perishable fruits, vegetables and grains that would be stored there for distribution or sale. He decided to add the control of natural air movement to the ancient local tactic of thermal mass, placing storage areas below grade, finding ways to improve wind-catch designs. In the market, which was built first, he was able to achieve dramatic temperature reductions of up to 15 degrees centigrade. In the housing, he combined these techniques with the double courtyard system he had appropriated from medieval Cairo to promote inductive cooling. This system links a hard paved court, which heats up during the day, with a planted courtyard next to it; the hot air rises by convection and cooler air 'stored' in the vegetation of the planted courtyard is drawn in through a *takhtabush*, or screen between the courtyards, creating a breeze.

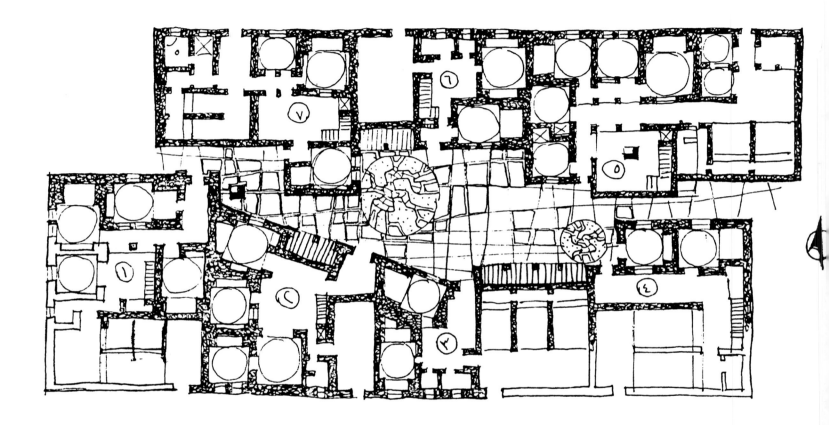

Above Sketch of a pedestrian street in New Baris, showing how interconnected houses can be built, each with their own individual courtyards, and still maintain private space. The idea of integrating animals stalls with the owner's living space (for example, bottom right of sketch) is familiar from New Gourna.

Opposite Vaulted pedestrian thoroughfare, New Baris market.

Following pages
Below right None of the housing at New Baris was ever completed; this small interior courtyard in the market gives an impression of how domestic courtyards might have looked.

Left and **above right** Fathy considered the market itself to be his highest achievement. Its undulating silhouette is a persuasive reminder that aesthetically pleasing forms can serve functional demands.

Unfortunately the disruption caused by war with Israel halted construction at New Baris in 1967, and it was not resumed. Recent plans to utilize the artesian well, in combination with a canal that will parallel the Nile along its entire extent from the Sudanese border to the Delta, may regenerate this visionary plan.

The last community project Fathy worked on was Dar al-Islam, located in Abiquiu, New Mexico. Initially envisaged as both a religious and educational as well as a residential centre, the community was intended for 100 families, as a model for others throughout the United States.

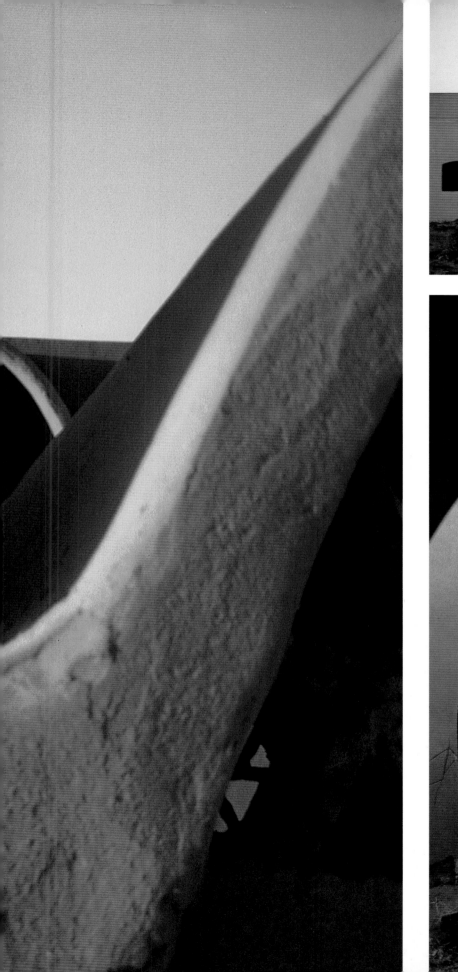

Opposite, above The mosque at Dar al-Islam, Abiquiu, New Mexico. Although Fathy wanted to explore established traditional Navajo building prototypes, he was encouraged to transplant the Nubian vault and dome idiom he had adopted in Egypt.

Opposite, below The methods taught by the Nubian masons who accompanied Fathy were not fully absorbed: expensive plywood forms had to be used. Costs increased, eventually causing the project to be curtailed.

Left and **below** Vaults and domes had to comply with strict American building codes: adobe, which had been used in this region for centuries, was classed as 'unstable' and had to be protected from the weather with a concrete skin. This required more elaborate foundations and construction requirements.

Interior of the mosque at Dar al-Islam, Abiquiu. The building combines Egyptian and local craftsmanship; the lanterns suspended from the dome are locally made.

Opposite Mosque at Dar al-Islam. Heavy seasonal rains in New Mexico made it necessary to install scuppers to direct water away from the concrete-coated mud brick.

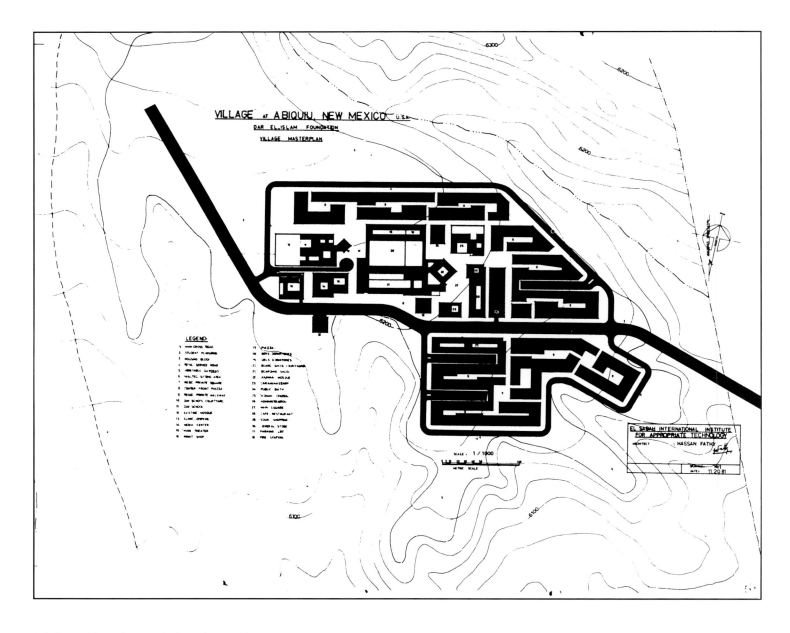

Fathy's original site plan, Dar al-Islam, Abiquiu. The mosque is in the centre.
The plan was changed after Fathy's death in 1989; several other architects
were invited to contribute to the project.

Opposite The construction of Dar al-Islam, Abiquiu. Fathy did not ask for
payment for his design proposals, out of piety. His presentation amounted to a
compelling summary of his architectural experience. When Fathy died in 1989,
only the mosque had been built.

The site comprises 1200 acres in the Chama River Valley fifty miles north of Santa Fe, in terrain similar to that in many Islamic countries in the Middle East. Fathy decided to make the mosque the heart of the community along with a religious school (*madrasa*) and living quarters for teachers (*riwaq*). The centre also includes an Institute for Advanced Islamic Studies, shops, a women's centre, library and clinic. In June 1980, Fathy visited the site, presenting his proposals which he designed without a fee, out of piety, and to demonstrate the traditional Nubian construction methods that he intended to use. He brought two Nubian masons with him to do so. He made his presentation to more than 300 people, including architects, builders and government officials from all over the United States, as well as future residents and community leaders. It evolved into a lecture that compressed Fathy's half century of hard-won experience into a summation of beliefs.

The themes of climate, cultural differences and finance determined the course of the project. Strict American building codes that rigidly classify adobe, which has been used in this region for centuries, as an unstable material that must be protected with a concrete skin, required more elaborate foundations and construction refinements than Fathy's self-help approach provided for, and social habits did not encourage co-operative building. These unanticipated differences caused costs to escalate, forcing financial backers in Saudi Arabia to reconsider their support and withdraw. All that had been built at the time of Fathy's death in 1989 was the 220 square metre mosque, standing as an evocative reminder of the spatial and structural possibilities that once existed.

The mosque complex, Dar al-Islam. The scale and structure bear familiar Fathy hallmarks; the unfamiliar concrete covering every surface gives the building a strangely artificial appearance. One of the vented vaults designed as a wind catch has been glazed, so that it provides light and prevents the infiltration of dust.

Opposite Entrance to the *madrasa* or religious school adjoining the mosque at Dar al-Islam.

153

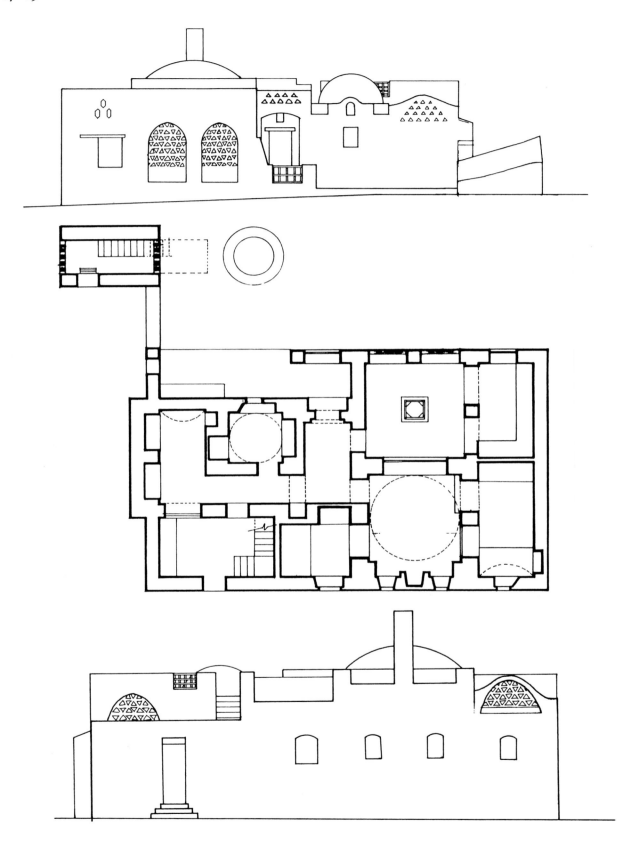

If the house an architect builds for himself provides an indication of his true character, Fathy's house at Sidi Krier reveals a complex personality within which a private, conservative side and an ebullient public face co-exist. It is the first example of his 'stone phase', a response to the ban on mud brick in parts of Egypt. Built of local limestone faced with plaster, the house demonstrated that his formal vocabulary and spatial thesis were not restricted to the use of a single material, but could adapt to local conditions, such as the natural stone outcrops and high humidity that exist here.

Fathy house, Sidi Krier. Built incrementally over several years from 1971, the house has an additive quality of careful balance. It continued to change for the rest of his life.

Opposite Early elevations and plan, Fathy's house at Sidi Krier. The elevation (at the top) faces the Mediterranean, and is open to breeze and views. The other side (elevation below) presents a more solid facade to the road. Over time, the side facing the water also became more closed as the surrounding area was built up.

Fathy's house, Sidi Krier. Characteristic pyramid-shaped openings serve to direct cooling draughts through the building; water in the vaulted well (**above left**) is also cooled by prevailing breezes. The two people in one of the outdoor 'rooms' (**below right**) give an impression of the building's intimate, human scale.

Opposite More than any other of Fathy's residential projects, the roof of the Sidi Krier house has been conceived as a series of outdoor 'rooms' and open courtyards, interconnected by stairs, and taking full advantage of Mediterranean views and breezes.

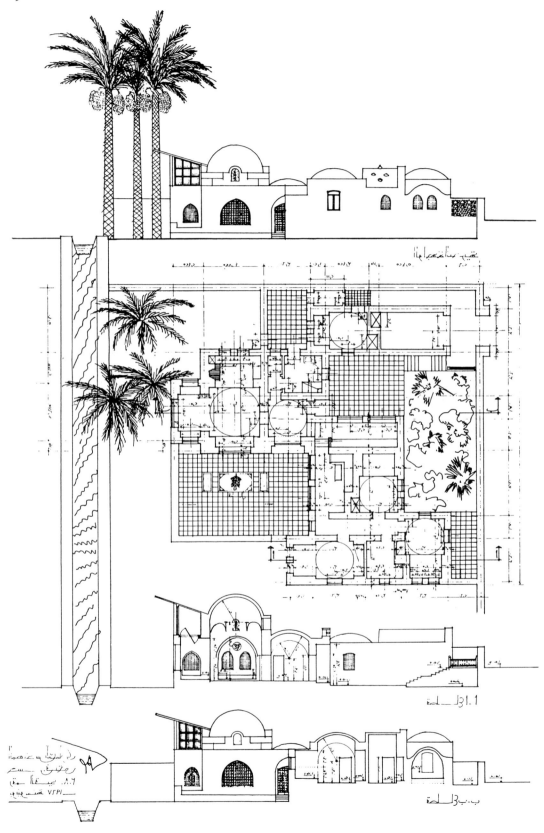

Elevation, plan and sections of the Fouad Riad house at Shabramant near Cairo.
The drawings indicate the unified vision Fathy had of the project.
The arrangement of formal volumes and spaces in plan is tightly controlled; the
drainage canal (left), fully grown palm trees and existing boundary wall (right)
imposed strict limitations, which Fathy was able to turn to advantage.

Less eccentric than it may at first seem, the house is lined up parallel with the shoreline with a blind side towards the public road running behind it and a more open face to the sea. The massing of the open side is much more compressed and intense than its blank public face with most dominant forms related to the vaults and cuneiform slots used to capture the cool ocean breeze.

The loggia, which is the outdoor equivalent of the inner *qa'a* and is separated from it by *mashrabiya* screens, is the primary space on this facade, and was originally intended to be open to the view. Fathy later added claustra-work inside its arches for greater privacy and an increased sense of enclosure, while not totally sacrificing the need for light, air and a feeling of the ocean beyond.

The roof of the house was also designed as a multi-level viewing platform and outdoor seating area that is accessible by stairs from the small entry courtyard on the public side of the property. The enclosed interior area is very restricted and compact, reflecting the architect's spartan habits and his desire to accentuate the use of complementary outdoor 'rooms'.

Fathy's house for Dr Fouad Riad was built in 1973. Begun as weekend retreat in much the same way as the Hamed Said house in Marg, the plan required the architect to allow for a fully grown stand of palm trees. While the site offers an impressive open view to the Giza Pyramids in the distance, planning was further complicated by the narrowness of the plot, which is restricted by a boundary wall on the road side and a drainage canal bordering the open fields beyond. To overcome these restrictions Fathy decided to engage the house more directly to the boundary wall in order to gain more private area in the rear of the house.

The torsional shift of grid that began to develop between the line of the road and the line of the building had usually only come about in Fathy's past work as a result of the directional imperatives of mosque design; it is also reminiscent of the spatial transitions between the public thoroughfare and building facades seen in Mamluk complexes such as the Qalawun Mausoleum in Old Cairo. Fathy's careful delineation of the exterior character of the house conveys a strong feeling of *misriya*, Egyptianness, due in part to the juxtaposition of a pigeon tower, *malkaf* (wind catch) and domed *qa'a* combination and extensive turned woodwork. Here, however, as in so much of the work done later in his career, the lack of a strong supervisory hand to carry out the architect's intent has resulted in many formal compromises and omissions that seriously detract from an authentically 'ethnic' image. Those omissions are probably also a logical extension of Fathy's basic belief that traditional forms have never come about through the efforts of an architect, but have emerged from the popular collective will.

As a result of this conflict, an emasculated *malkaf* remains as a single forlorn fin wall, looking as if the decision not to complete it was made after it was begun. Similarly, although the stonework does not correspond to the smooth image originally conveyed in the drawings, there are indications that masonry techniques were changed after Fathy had visited some villages by the Red Sea where stone rather than mud brick is used extensively, and where 25 by 15 by 15 centimetre blocks are laid up rough and dry.

Fouad Riad house, Shabramant, near Cairo. After visiting some villages by the Red Sea, Fathy decided to use stone instead of mud brick. Although the original intention was to plaster over the surface, the walls and vaults have been left exposed.

Opposite The *maqa'ad* (loggia) also serves to shade the windows overlooking the garden.

Below The *umriyad* set into the dome provides an effective light source without generating much heat inside.

Views of the Fouad Riad house, Shabramant, near Cairo.

Below right The *maqa'ad* of the Fouad Riad house appears as two vaulted alcoves facing out onto an internal garden. The house is strategically sited to block out noise from the road.

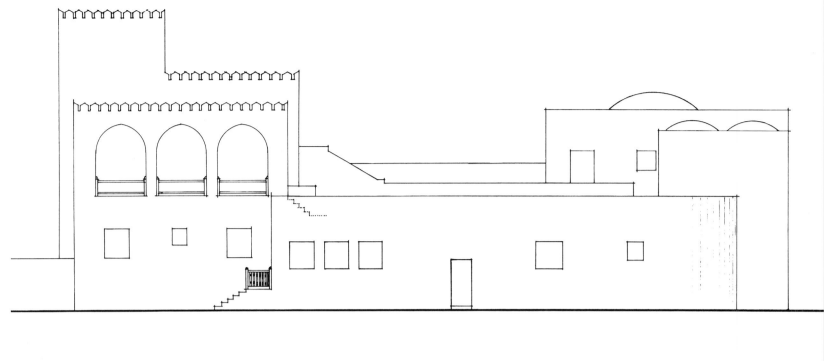

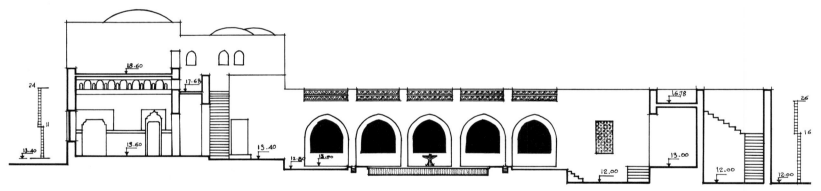

Elevation and section, Alpha Bianca house, Majorca. The house was based on a desert fortress of the type built at the time of Moorish influence in Majorca. The section (below) shows the stepped floor levels.

Opposite Plan of Alpha Bianca house. Circulation weaves in and out of spaces surrounding the protected inner courtyard. The steps in the drawing indicate the frequent change of floor level.

Alpha Bianca, built by Fathy for the artists Yannick Vu and Ben Jackober in Majorca, is based on the *ribat* or fortified palace most commonly found in North Africa, a type of building not used in the Arab world for centuries. The design evolved from the owners' idea of enclosing an existing rectangular terrace on a fifty-acre site in the northwest corner of the island. They decided to break the terrace down into various levels; the stepped patios began to suggest a Moorish theme to them, which seemed very appropriate since the Moors had once used Palma as a stronghold.

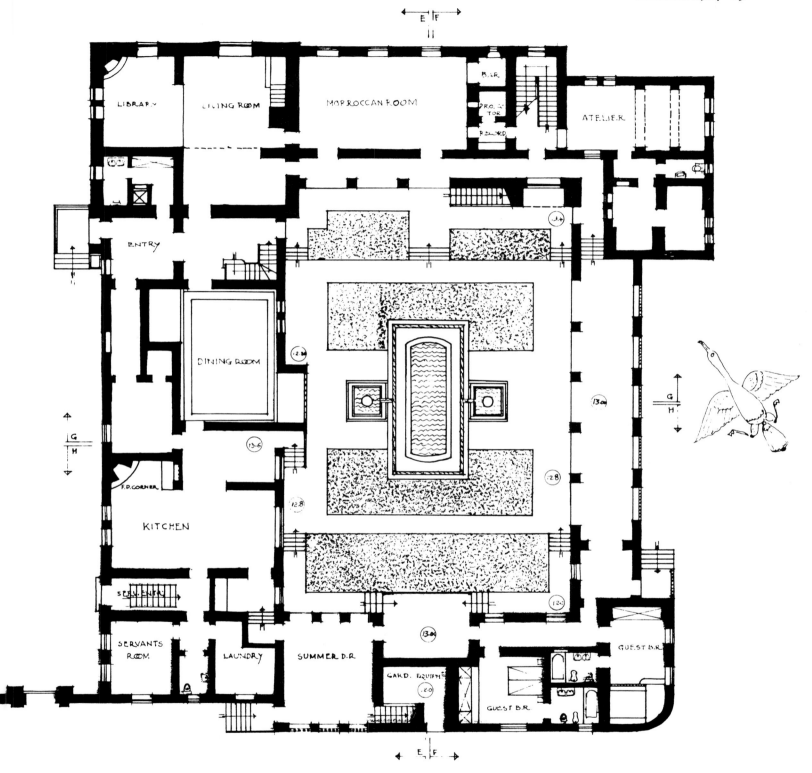

LIBRARY

LIVING ROOM

MOROCCAN ROOM

BAR

PROJECTOR

RECORD

ATELIER

ENTRY

DINING ROOM

KITCHEN

F.P. CORNER

SERVANTS ROOM

LAUNDRY

SUMMER D.R.

GARD. EQUIP.

GUEST B.R.

GUEST B.R.

Andrioli house, Fayyum. Situated at the crest of a hill, the construction of the house was carefully controlled by the owner, who made significant alterations to the original plan. The vividly painted solid wooden shutters replace the more costly *mashrabiya* Fathy proposed.

Above The side facing the road is solid, in contrast to the open arcade on the other side, which overlooks a palm grove, a lake in the valley, and beyond to the desert.

Right and **opposite** The main dome has been built lower than originally designed, in order to fit more comfortably with the neighbouring buildings in the village.

The stylistic direction and general form of the *ribat* was already roughly set when Fathy received the commission. He began to organize the spaces around three sides of the 17 by 25 metre courtyard, reserving the fourth side for a deep arcade. The long open interior atrium was used to further advantage to segregate the family quarters at one end and the guest and service rooms at the other, linked by the kitchen, dining room and entry between. All rooms extend large windows, usually covered with *mashrabiya* screens, to the interior atrium, while exterior windows are minimized.

As usual in Fathy's work the house as built shows major changes from the preliminary plans and elevations, but the basic concept remains intact, with only the detailing of domes and crenellations having been altered. The scale and terracing of the interior courtyard have remained constant, however, realizing a self-contained world that stands in sharp contrast to the rugged wooded slopes beyond the walls.

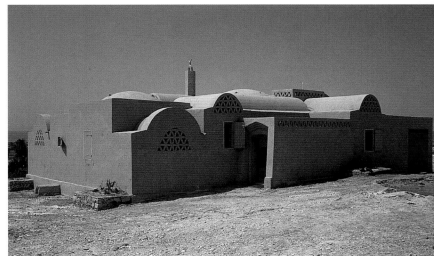

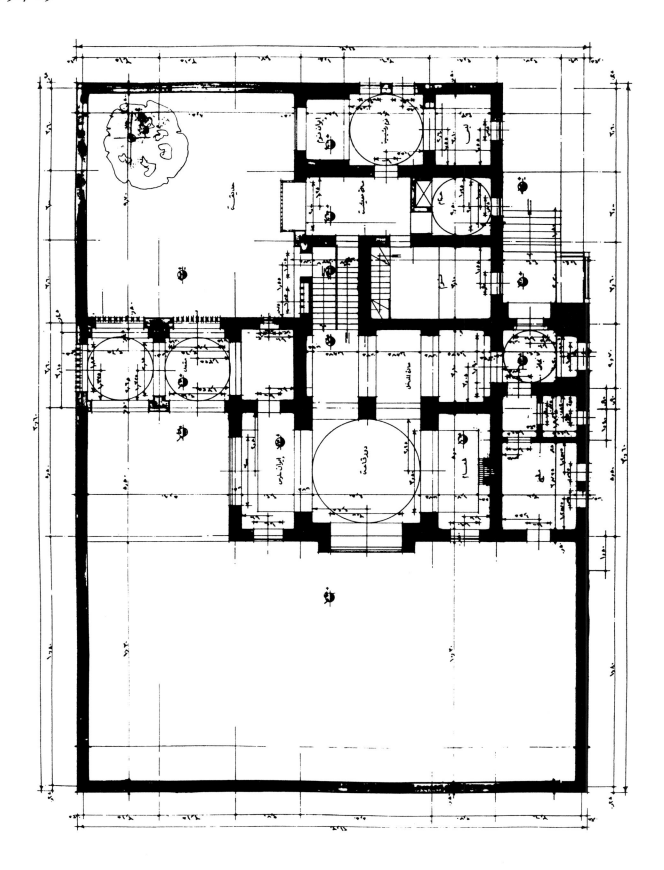

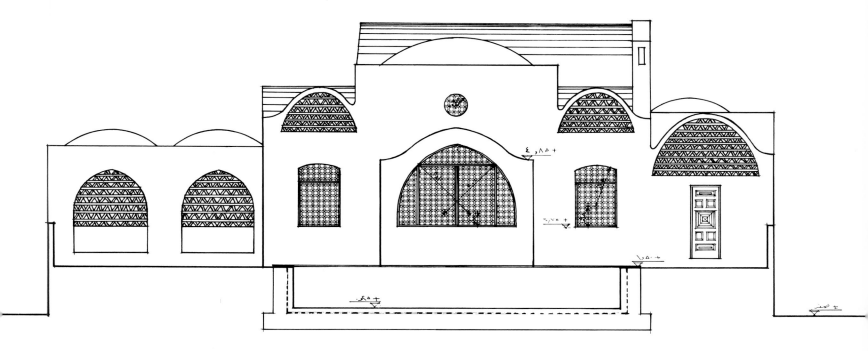

The house Fathy built for Dr and Mrs Murad Greiss was finished in 1984. With its chalky white Muqattam and Helwan limestone finish, shallow dome and bubble picture window overlooking a kidney-shaped swimming pool, it stands in sharp contrast to the golden earth tones of the Fouad Riad house. The basic spatial arrangement remains constant, however, with an indirect entry leading into a formal *qa'a*. This *qa'a*, with flanking *iwans* facing into a 'hard' paved courtyard (with pool, in this case), is separated from the 'soft' planted courtyard by a *takhtabush*. Fathy adds novelty to these now standard relationships by tightly organizing them into a spiralling boundary wall and then introducing an artificially raised plinth into the formal reception area and pool court to differentiate it from the private family sleeping and studio area.

The Sheikh Nasser al-Sabah house, designed for the Fentas area of Kuwait, was one of Fathy's last major projects; commissioned in 1982, it is still not complete. This house offers one of the best opportunities to study the consistent set of principles used by the architect throughout his career in the final stage of their

Elevation (**above**) and plan (**opposite**) of the Murad Greiss house, 1982. The double-domed *takhtabush* on the left, extended at right angles to the *qa'a*, is a distinctive feature. It is used as a breezy, shaded seating area between a small courtyard and large garden. The line of the boundary wall spirals clockwise into the heart of the house.

evolution, and to make comparisons with his earliest houses. The *magaz*, the central courtyard, the *maqa'ad*, the vaulted gallery, and the strict division between public and private space are all present here in highly visible form due to the large scale of the project.

What first becomes obvious in the plan is the formal separation of the house into two distinct volumes, clearly related to the public and private functions of the interior. These two volumes are separated by an axial wall that allowed the architect to offset each of these areas to allow a large principal entrance for guests at the top of the plan. This entrance leads into a long gallery that was originally intended to be a *majlis* for guests, supported by two high pointed arches related to the projecting buttresses on its side. Unlike other instances in the past where such a gallery has been used, as in the Hamed Said and Stopplaere houses for example, where

Opposite and above Murad Greiss house, Shabramant outside Cairo.
Like the Akil Sami house built nearby (**below**), the Murad Greiss house
demonstrates the versatility of Fathy's proven vault and dome construction
when combined with other load-bearing materials – the use of mud brick
was now legally restricted. Both of these late designs demonstrate Fathy's
assured and skilful handling of forms and materials at the peak of his career.

171

Section and elevations of the al-Sabah house, Fentas, Kuwait, 1982.
One of the largest private commissions Fathy ever undertook, the house has a
carefully divided interior, built around three open courtyards – public, private
and intermediary. *Mashrabiya* are used extensively to complement other natural
ventilation. A high octagonal structure sits above the *qa'a*, in place of the more
usual dome, and contrasts with the delicate forms of the slatted wooden
pergola (**bottom, right**) which shades a fourth courtyard.

it was introduced as a buffer space linking different zones and providing an innovative solution to what might otherwise have been a simple utilitarian corridor, this gallery is located on an outside wall and ends abruptly. Long, narrow windows covered with *mashrabiya* screens are placed between the buttresses that support the roof to allow filtered light to stream into the room, further punctuating the movement through it toward the stair at its opposite end. This stair, in turn, leads to the first floor and *maqa'ad* above, which is placed in front of a string of rooms lining the exterior wall, and separated from them by a long narrow corridor. This corridor runs past the wide opening into the *maqa'ad*, making it unmistakably recognizable as a unique space among all of the others on this level, as do the solid walls that bracket each of its sides. A second stair leads along one of these walls, and then turns at a right angle toward the main courtyard below in a way often seen in houses like the Bayt Suhaymi in medieval Cairo, which presents a classical elevation to those looking up from below.

The rooms behind the *maqa'ad*, which were originally intended to be service kitchens for the *majlis* below, have now been converted into libraries that house a small portion of the owner's extensive collection of books and provide quiet places for reading and study away from the more active areas of the house. The *maqa'ad* overlooks the first and largest of three inner courtyards in the house that are each open to the sky and move in rhythmic progression from the upper middle to lower right part of the plan.

The long, arched gallery on the upper side of this public zone is evenly balanced by a fourth, covered court and finally by the *qa'a* along side it, which is the highest space in the house. The *qa'a* is also accompanied by a *malkaf*, and is located next to the wall dividing the public and private zones of the house. This complimentary pairing of a perfectly square, pergola-covered court and a *qa'a* covered by a *shukshaykha* (vented lantern dome) appropriately completes this series of spaces that begins with a *majlis* and ends in a room that stands for hospitality itself. The pergola over the fourth small court here deserves special note for its similarity to another designed for the Monastirli house in 1950. In that instance, a court that is almost a mirror image of this one was placed at the top of a monumental stair leading up to the bedrooms on the upper floor, which are grouped around it. Delicate wooden slats are used in both cases to create a bell-shaped tent that casts lacy shadows onto the tiled floor below. Abdel Wahed el-Wakil has also used this concept in the Suliman Palace in Jeddah, Saudi Arabia, in a central court that pays homage to the Monastirli house and predates Fathy's nostalgic repetition of this form in highly compatible combination used here. A stair of the same proportion as the one going down from the *maqa'ad* to the central court also leads out from this covered court to a long narrow terrace that faces the Arabian Gulf and provides a place to sit and enjoy the view during those months in Kuwait when the weather is not oppressive. The heavy walls of the *qa'a* finally culminate in an octagonal *shukshaykha*, rather than the domed *qa'a* that is so closely identified with Fathy's earlier work. The reasons behind its selection here may relate to the fact that the *shukshaykha* has fewer specifically regional associations than the dome, which may also account for its use in the Abdallah Nassif house, as well as for another

173

Although not all of Fathy's late projects were built according to his original plans, they all bear the distinctive features that he had first conceived fifty years earlier; and they not only visibly link his buildings with the traditional architecture of Egypt, but to broader associations with Islam, via their symbolic domed forms.

Above Talhuni house, Amman, Jordan, 1988.

Opposite, above and **this page, below** Hassan Rashad house, near Ibiar, Tanta, 1989.

Opposite, below Resthouse located in the desert region near Aswan for use by President Anwar Sadat during inspection tours of Upper Egypt, 1981.

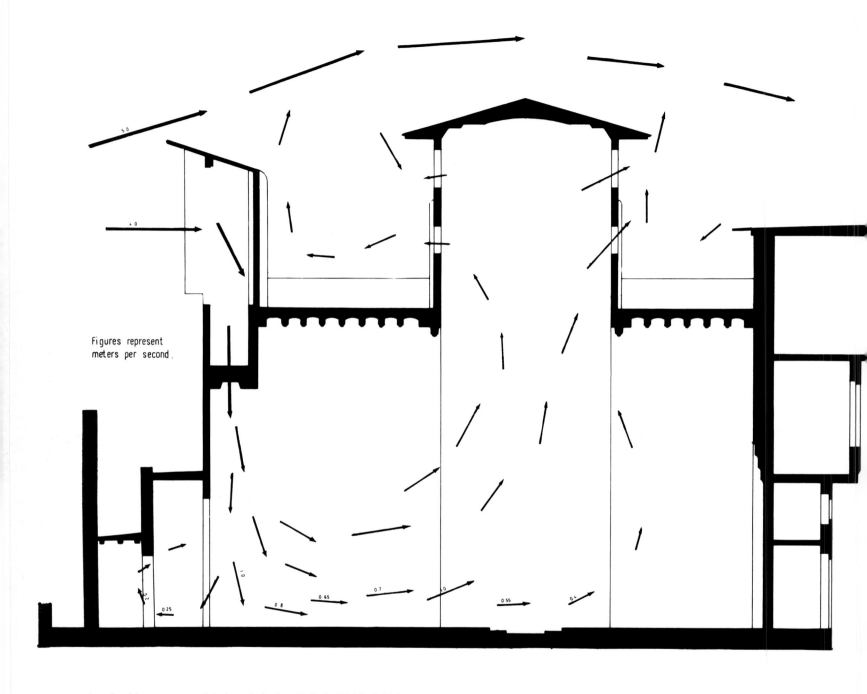

Figures represent meters per second.

A study of the movement of air through the Bayt Kathoda (Mohib al-Din) by a team from the Architectural Association, London, which included Omar el-Farouk. The prevailing northeasterly wind enters the *malkaf* and cools the interior space. Warmer air rises and disperses through the *shukshaykha* (vented lantern dome) above the *qa'a*.

designed for Tabuk, both in Saudi Arabia. The shallow angles of the *shukshaykha* have a particular elegance all of their own, which allows other forms, such as the delicate pergola nearby, to emerge as individual elements in their own right, rather than being subservient to more dominant members of the same tectonic family.

A single stair attached to the *malkaf* links this complete formal enclosure with the private world that compliments it on the other side of the central dividing wall. As in the reception zone, central courtyards also serve as points of orientation. Rather than having all rooms surrounding the central court as before, however, Fathy breaks these courts down in scale to relate to the more intimate and domestic character of this area. The more centrally located of the two courts that are used in this way is directly connected to the children's bedroom area. These are grouped along an exterior wall around it, and end in a sitting room that overlooks the large central court of the formal zone through a projecting *mashrabiya* screen that penetrates the massive dividing wall. These bedrooms, which have a bath of their own, each have a square central space covered by a low dome, with a lower sleeping *iwan* related to it. This provides a change of scale within the bedroom, and allows each one to be more comfortable. In contrast to the children's bedrooms, the master bedroom suite has a longer rectilinear courtyard that serves as its inner focus, and effectively terminates the line of circulation joining the children's rooms together. This longer court is placed between a three-bay-wide sitting area which has a screened vista of the gulf on the one hand, and the master bedroom and bath on its inner edge. Both areas look into the court

The roof of the fifteenth-century Bayt Kathoda, Cairo. Visible are the *malkaf* and *shukshaykha*.

and receive light from it. The protective walls of this last grouping of rooms seem to echo those of the large formal *qa'a* adjacent to it, in the way they turn inward and provide *iwans* for relaxation and sleeping.

The al-Sabah house is far more than a fitting finale to Hassan Fathy's career; it is an object lesson in the principles that he adhered to and a lasting testimony to their effectiveness. Each segment of his highly personal spatial and structural language is present here, often repeated like the musical fugues he loved so much. This repetition only helps to amplify his intentions in the use of each in earlier projects and serves as a guide for their implementation throughout his entire career. Rather than using only one open court as he

177

Akil Sami house, Shabramant, Cairo. Fathy's deployment of shade and ventilation is especially refined here; the *takhtabush* draws breeze through the perforations in the right-hand wall.

Opposite Murad Greiss house, Shabramant, Cairo. Although the vaults were originally designed to provide ventilation, these were glazed over to prevent the infiltration of dust.

frequently did in his early work, for example, he uses three to indicate a diagonal line between the most important public space in one corner of the house and the most private at the opposite extreme. The fourth court brings back memories of another time and place, masterfully preparing those about to experience the vertical drama of the *qa'a* by first offering them the fragile canopy of a wooden dome instead. The *maqa'ad* is classical in proportion, orientation and detailing, serving as a textbook example of this particular kind of space. In a manner that vividly recalls the paving patterns used in the intermediate plan of the Hamdi Seif al-Nasr house that he designed nearly a half century before, those in the al-Sabah house were originally intended to provide an individual sense of scale, human reference and visual measurement. Each was a work of art never to be repeated, worked out inside the frame of its own particular space. Every element can be seen as the culmination of the lessons learned in all of his past work, used with loving care.

For young architects all over the world, the search for a traditional language seems to represent a direct threat to their creativity and individuality; and yet, the al-Sabah house clearly shows that no such threat exists. Rather than restricting Fathy's creativity, the language that he evolved from his studies of the past gave him more freedom to use that language in even more eloquent ways. While staying firmly within the confines of his cultural heritage, he also managed to provide a residence with a contemporary and international character that is totally in keeping with the high level of sophistication and wide-ranging, cosmopolitan interests of the owners.

Conclusion

assan Fathy's remarkable achievements must be assessed against both the record of implementation of his ideas and the more measured view taken of area studies at the close of the 1990s. It is also instructive to consider his work in conjunction with *Orientalism*, the landmark study of the objectification of a culture written by Edward W. Said in 1978.

It took more than a decade, to a point roughly coinciding with Fathy's death in 1989, for Said's arguments to gain international currency and they continue to be debated among anthropologists, ethnographers, historians, and sociologists. They have particular relevance in the case of Hassan Fathy, however, because of his singular position as a translator of tradition. As a means of interpretation of the civilizations, peoples, and localities of what was popularly called the Orient, Said defines Orientalism as 'a system of representation framed by a whole set of forces that brought the Orient into western learning, western consciousness and, later, western empire.'[1] Said's principle assumption is that such learning was subject to social and cultural constraints, traditions, and aspirations and in its last manifestation became 'a racist, an imperialist, and almost totally ethnocentric' system used by Europeans to suppress 'other' cultures during the colonial era.[2]

Fathy's primary sources and methodology were indelibly influenced by the phenomenon that Said describes. Fathy was the product of a British colonial educational system, based on the French Ecole des Beaux-Arts; and the literary sources upon which he initially relied most heavily were those held at the Institut Français Archaeologique Orientale in Cairo, a prime example of the institutionalization of representation that Said describes.[3] Because these shaped his attitudes and filtered his aesthetic vision, they must be objectively reviewed and understood.

Said bases his study on Michel Foucault's methodology of a 'discourse', but his is extended into a non-ethnocentric, more general exploration to include the way, as Clifford James describes it, 'in which a cultural order is defined externally, with respect to exotic others.'[4] In Said's view, the representation of subject peoples and places by agents and institutions of colonial governments is comparable to class division in European nations as described by Foucault as a means of imposing power, 'physical and ideological' discipline, and confinement.[5] Said defines the 'scope of Orientalism', 'Orientalist structures and restructures' and the state of 'Orientalism now', but restricts himself to British and French colonial definitions of the Arab Middle East, significantly excluding Asia and North Africa, as well as German, Spanish, Italian, and Russian

Orientalist literature. These omissions are rectified in his *Culture and Imperialism*, which followed in 1993.

In tracing the beginning of the objectification of the Orient, Said describes how important Egypt was in the colonial schema, not just as a material holding, but as a 'vindication' of the entire system. Britain used Egypt as a paragon of development; England's representative, Lord Cromer, in a speech to the House of Commons in 1907, stated that Egypt had been raised, since the time of its occupation in 1892, 'from the lowest pitch of social and economic degradation until it now stands among Oriental nations, I believe, absolutely alone in its prosperity, financial and moral.'[6] Said presents Orientalism as a systematized effort to contain another culture by claiming to be able to represent it accurately in written or graphic form.

The Napoleonic campaign of 1798 was recorded in the *Description de l' Egypte*, which was the result of an academic invasion that took place in concert with the military expedition it accompanied. Published in 23 enormous folios between 1809 and 1828, the *Description* was nothing less than an attempt to document comprehensively the historical artifacts, urban settlements, biology, botany, geology, and ethnography of an entire nation; to contain it taxonometrically and by containing, to capture it. The field of Egyptology originated in this effort, and the discovery of the Rosetta Stone allowed hieroglyphics to be deciphered for the first time by Jean-François Champollion.

Five hundred civilians accompanied Napoleon, including 167 scholars, 21 mathematicians, 3 astronomers, 17 civil engineers, 13 naturalists, 4 architects, 8 draughtsmen and 22 printers. They were stranded in Egypt after Napoleon destroyed two hundred of the ships that had conveyed the expedition there at the Battle of Abukir and were left to fend for themselves when their general returned to France after winning the Battle of the Pyramids on 21 July, 1798. With the British navy in control of the port of Alexandria, it is remarkable that any of the drawings made it back to Paris intact. They were almost burned by the French to avoid confiscation, but escaped capture. All objects were seized by the British, and the one-metre square, 762-kilo Rosetta Stone is now in the British Museum as a result. Once safely at the Imperial Press, it took 400 engravers to transfer the drawings onto copper plates and 20 years to produce the folios. The architects in the expedition recorded a way of life that was soon to vanish because of rulers who wanted to make Egypt 'a part of Europe', etching a plan of the medieval quarter of Cairo, making extensive drawings of Azbekiah, Birkit al-Fil, the Citadel, walls, and private houses. This rare documentation, later supplemented by a record of the much reduced remnant by Panty and Prisse d'Avennes, was the equivalent of a guide book for Fathy in his search for an authentic national architectural language, but the architectural portion, like the rest, was typologically organized and conceived.

Said contends that it was the attitude displayed in this ambitious enterprise rather than its unprecedented scale, which is most important, since it consists of a 'textural' attack on an alien culture, lifting Egypt from the 'realms of silent obscurity … into the clarity of modern European science …. Quite literally, the occupation gave birth to the entire modern experience of the Orient.'[7] Napoleon's agenda was not purely academic. Said shows that his model was the *Voyage en*

Egypte et en Syrie, written by the Comte de Volney in 1787, a thinly disguised reconnaissance preceding French colonial purpose, which enumerated the difficulties that any expedition would encounter. Volney listed three enemies that France would face in an attempt to conquer Egypt: the Ottoman Empire, England, and Islam. For all Napoleon's professed sympathy for Muslim culture and sincere admiration of the Qur'an, the *Description de l'Egypte* may be regarded as a sophisticated battle plan against Islam, with the full weight of governmental and academic sanction behind it. The *Description* took on the aura of great authority, the crucial paradox that Foucault identifies, of text creating the reality it describes in addition to the knowledge it is intended to convey.

The tradition that it established, of scientific knowledge being put to political use, may be identified in Fathy's method. 'Arab architects' can thus be isolated as an object of study, as a historical entity, described with insight by Anwar Abd al-Malik as 'thematic, …an essentialist conception of the countries, nations, and peoples of the Orient under study, a conception which expresses itself through a characterized ethnist typology'. This thematism is curiously ahistorical, since it obviates the subtleties that accrue through interaction between various cultures, religions, and periods. Thus, 'one ends with a typology – based on a real specificity, but detached from history and, consequently, conceived as being intangible, essential.'[8]

It is important to recall that at about the same time that Napoleon returned to France from Egypt, Jean Nicholas Durand (1760–1854) had just published his first book, *Recueil et Parallele des Edifices de Tout Genre, Anciens et Modernes* (1799), in which he classifies an extensive selection of historical and contemporary buildings according to period, function and form. In it, he extends the ideas of his teacher, Jacques-François Blondel, best remembered for his concept of *caractère* (character), related to the honest expression of structure, form, and function. This was to become a central principle in the Ecole des Beaux-Arts that he helped to found. Durand was as systematic as his mentor, with one significant difference: he rejected entirely the Aristotelean concept of mimesis, or imitation, that tied classical architecture to nature, the column to the tree that preceded it. In this move, he divorced rational architecture and type from nature. Durand initiated the transfer of categories, classifying architecture in the same way as species in the natural sciences, seeking general similarities rather than singular eccentricities. In the classification of type, as well as species, the goal was to extract 'general principles from particular cases', and Durand established four rules to do this: 'According to the first rule, the first step is to recognize what defines architecture in a way that cannot be denied, that is to say to start with the study of existing buildings.'[9] The second rule is to define fundamental elements, the third to synthesize those elements to be able to see them in creating a new building, and the fourth is to determine how they may be recombined in new compositional arrangements. Durand taught at the Polytechnique, not at the Ecole des Beaux-Arts, and his *Précis* of lessons was published soon after. Kenneth Frampton has traced what he terms Le Corbusier's 'Classical Machinism' or Purism to

French Classical Rationalism in as much as it terminated a trajectory of thought running from

J. N. L. Durand's *Précis des Leçons Données à l'Ecole Polytechnique* of 1801–5 to Julien Guadet's *Eléments et Théorie de l'Architecture* of 1902. Le Corbusier was to absorb this heritage through Perret and Garnier, both of whom had been star pupils of Julien Guadet during his tenure as professor of theory at the Ecole des Beaux-Arts.[10]

In an article about his friend in one of two initial studies on Hassan Fathy that appeared in 1988, J. M. Richards caused a storm of protest among followers by suggesting that his functionalism and clear expression of form, structure, and materials put Fathy on a parallel path with Modernism, regardless of the historical elements he chose to reinterpret. Fathy's followers were, and still are, outraged at such a notion since they respond to his stated intentions, as expressed in his writing, teaching and public lectures, rather than dispassionately analysing his methodology. Fathy pronounced against the tacit acceptance of a culturally anonymous international style for the sake of technological progress, and particularly against what he characterized as the arrogance of Le Corbusier's insistence on the use of expensive industrial materials in developing contexts where they were technically, financially and environmentally inappropriate. This makes it seem inconceivable that Fathy would use the same methods he professed to abhor. And yet, Richards can only be faulted for not going far enough. He did not consider the causes of Orientalist intimidation that fostered cultural envy and insecurity, or the separation into rational typology that is one of the founding tenets of Modernism that derived, almost subconsciously, from such typological discourse. Fathy was a victim of the syndrome most clearly defined as 'marginality' (being between Arab and Western culture) by Jacques Berque, one of his favourite writers, a syndrome now increasingly identified as a global epidemic in our increasingly interconnected world. He was proud of his Arab heritage and wanted to preserve and defend it against further foreign intrusion, and yet he also admired the alien culture he blamed for this corruption.

Fathy was a product of the Ecole des Beaux-Arts tradition, which also produced Durand, Guadet and Le Corbusier. On a more personal level, he conversed enthusiastically in French, had many European friends, played Brahms, wore Savile Row suits, and observed tea time, which he continued in four o'clock afternoon receptions in his studio until illness finally prevented him from carrying out the daily ritual. Clifford James has updated Berque's definition of marginality to apply to a global constituency, calling it the predicament of culture

> that responds to the twentieth century's unprecedented overlay of traditions. A modern ethnography of conjunctures, constantly moving between cultures … is perpetually displaced, both regionally focused and broadly comparative, a form both of dwelling and of travel in a world where the two experiences are less and less distinct.[11]

This may also serve as a precise description of Fathy's dilemma: both as 'citizen of the world' and as self-styled champion of his own cultural tradition, he promoted what he thought was a genuine discovery of an indigenous Egyptian architecture, rendered in mud – historically and environmentally an appropriate and plentiful material.

It is now clear that Fathy's 'thesis of space', which he derived from his studies of the Mamluk and Ottoman *manzils* (great houses) in the medieval quarter of Cairo, is strictly typological and many of those he analysed are also classified in the *Description de l'Egypte*. One can appreciate his sense of discovery when he realized that there are similar elements in the surviving, but rapidly vanishing houses that have evolved out of the specific social and environmental conditions of Cairo. His subsequent, extensive studies on some of these spaces, such as the *qa'a* and the courtyard, indicate his level of enthusiasm and commitment.[12] The more important question, which is almost impossible to determine, is the extent with which he was *pre-disposed* by his early training to look for such elements in his eagerness to establish a viable alternative cultural identity and personal reputation. This issue of cultural 'infection' is also the implied core of Said's *Orientalism*: what *is* the proper way to search for authenticity and is it possible to find it following post-industrial cross-fertilization? 'Can one', as Clifford James asks, 'ultimately escape procedures of dichotomizing, restructuring, and textualizing in the making of interpretive statements about foreign cultures and traditions?'[13] And how can such dichotomizing be avoided when the foreign culture under study happens to be your own?

A graphic example of this difficulty arose in a lecture at the Royal Academy in June 1995 by renowned Japanese architect Arata Isozaki. He poignantly described the growing recognition among Japanese architects that precious traditions in his country – which has individualized and perpetuated them more recognizably than many other nations – are being irretrievably lost. He also admitted that non-Japanese, who often regard Japanese culture as mysterious and indecipherable, look to interlocutors such as him, to do so. But he claimed that Japanese culture is as foreign to him as it is to outsiders, and that this could be attributed to the wholesale assimilation of Western culture and technology after the Second World War, which deeply affected his entire generation. In spite of this striking recognition, Isozaki has been as persistently courageous in his search for a true expression of Japanese culture as Fathy was in trying to determine what is authentically Egyptian. In retrospect, Fathy's 'thesis of space' typology is derived from the Enlightenment tradition and is selective since it was derived primarily from those models specifically indicated in the *Description de l'Egypte*.

Reversing Said's argument about the objective representation of the Orient, it is just as difficult and equally inaccurate to hold the West responsible – as Fathy and his followers have done – for a wide variety of social ills, ranging from the erosion of social values to urban desecration. Fathy's ability to categorize 'the West' as an objective entity demonstrates his reflectiveness in regard to 'the Orient.' It is indicative of his ability to be abstract about his own culture, as well.

One of the most remarkable effects of Fathy's legacy, of ideas as well as buildings, is the amount of confusion that exists about this issue of representation and authenticity. The question of representation, or the means used to achieve it, is relative to Fathy's own cultural awareness. His primary disciple, Abdel Wahed el-Wakil, is a case in point, complicating the issue of typology even further. In an extensive series of projects, beginning in Egypt in the early 1970s and continuing in Saudi Arabia later in the decade and on into the early 1980s, el-Wakil amplified his mentor's 'thesis of space', overlaying it with a concerted attempt at unravelling the geometric puzzle of Islamic detailing in elements such as the *muqarnas*, or stalactite moulding used in the *qibla* niche of a mosque or above doorways or windows as an elaboration of an arch. Fathy's focus on identifying what he considered to be appropriate and valid syntactical elements from Islamic architecture in the past to be recycled into a contemporary language has been sharpened by el-Wakil to include details, as well, and he reproduces these with consummate skill. El-Wakil began by implementing what Fathy had perfected. The courtyard, or frequently a double courtyard to induce convective cooling, the *qa'a*, *iwan*, *magaz*, *maqa'ad*, *takhtabush* and windcatch, are all evident in the Halawa House in Agami, Egypt, which won el-Wakil an Aga Khan Award in 1978 and brought him international recognition.

More funding for research and development that followed el-Wakil's move to Jeddah allowed him to pursue his interest in geometry and to explore the theory behind its application in Islamic architecture, relative to the Qur'anic injunction against representation, to an extent that Fathy never was able to accomplish. The need for familial privacy, and a concerted effort to update the historical Jeddah tower house, a relatively small walled enclosure that existed until the mid-1940s which had evolved to adapt to a humid climate with stratified ocean breezes, led to the Suliman Palace of 1976. It is essentially the Jeddah tower house turned 180 degrees, stretched out horizontally into similar public and private zones to adapt to the contemporary condition in Saudi Arabia of a detached villa centred on a large lot. Inside this linear revision of a historical form, el-Wakil has implemented Fathy's language in the unlikely juxtaposition of architectural elements used by wealthy merchants in thirteenth-, fourteenth- and fifteenth-century Cairo, here in the twentieth-century villa of a Saudi sheikh.

'Tradition is the social equivalent of personal habit.' Fathy made a transition from this statement in *Architecture for the Poor* to the facile assimilation of building for a completely different way of life. This can be explained on symbolic, rather than functional, grounds. The selection of Fathy to design the Dar al-Islam community in Abiquiu, New Mexico, is an example of the extent of his success in identifying emotive symbols. He logically argued that this was a regional historical tradition unfamiliar to him, but his patrons did not choose him for his ability to interpret Navajo architecture. He was specifically expected to provide the same dome and vault semiotics with which he had become identified in the half century he had employed them. These have become symbols of rebellion against the establishment, against a patent acceptance of the concept of progress at any price. They have also come to represent cultural autonomy and environmental and contextual sensitivity, instead of global homogeneity devoid of context. Through a complex set of cultural circumstances, Fathy's vaults and domes may seem to indicate the shift toward fundamentalism. Tradition is most distilled in religion, making him the logical choice to confer architectural legitimacy as one of the largest Muslim communities to ever be established in the United States, in spite of the fact that his typologies are once again inappropriate to their time, function, and location. Unlike el-Wakil's Jeddah transplants, this disjunction had serious repercussions in America, where the notion of self-help translates into 'help yourself' and temperature swings are more severe than in the Middle East. Unlike the Sa'idi at New Gourna, who were reluctant for entirely different reasons, the American clients wanted the image, but not the work necessary to achieve it or the maintenance schedule needed to uphold it. The assumption that the inhabitants would be unwilling to renew the mud-brick construction with a waterproof plaster coating every year led local legislators to enforce building codes requiring a concrete coating even before the project was submitted.

The enduring power of representation and its transfer into symbolism is also evident in el-Wakil's King Saud Mosque, which was built in accordance with Fathy's regenerated Nubian techniques. El-Wakil is fond of recounting the story of how he insisted that the dome, with a span exceeding 20 metres, be built without centring support, following Fathy's principles. This decision had serious ramifications, since building failure resulting in injury or death can result in a demand for an equivalent punishment from the family of the person affected under the *lex talionis* (law of retaliation) of the Shariah. Finding masons wasn't easy under such circumstances and el-Wakil wears his ability to overcome such difficulties as a badge of honour, having adhered to his, or Fathy's, principles at the risk of death.

With the temporary departure of Abdel Wahed el-Wakil from his practice in London in the late 1980s, Jordanian architect Rasem Badran began to assume prominence as the leading champion of Fathy's ideas. Significantly, he has also adopted a typological approach, but rather than restricting his analysis and selection to Egyptian models and details, as Fathy and el-Wakil have, he has laid comprehensive claim to the entire iconography of Islam as it relates to each country for which he designs. His approach is more heuristic than others, dependent on clues offered by existing context, but ends up being equally selective. Before he begins design, Badran makes exhaustive sketch studies of regional historical examples and then bases his forms on them. In this way, a Chamber of Commerce in Damman, Saudi Arabia, is conceived with chambered walls that replace the ventilation slots in older buildings and with a wind catch used for symbolic, as well as functional, reasons. A mosque in Riyadh becomes an opportunity to explore the relationship between sacred and secular architecture in the urban fabric and to return to the symbiotic relationship that existed before large congregational mosques became insular objects, isolated in the middle of large parking lots. A housing project in Yemen is based on typologies commonly found in rural villages and towns, such as the central court, communal well, local mosque, private garden, and vertical layering in each residence, moving from public to private, just as it did in the homes that el-Wakil observed in Jeddah.

The extensive influence that these two leading disciples of Hassan Fathy continue to exert throughout the Middle East and in the international Islamic community is a vital indication of their mentor's enormous contribution to filling a vacuum that existed in a particular area of cultural expression and identity. The contradictions inherent in the framework that he and they have used in their search for such expression, while problematic, are finally less important than the perception that this diversity can find a means of expression and need not rely on an alien culture to do so. Hassan Fathy is directly responsible for that realization and the sense of empowerment he has initiated has now begun to reverberate throughout the developing world. He offers an example to others who have felt defeated by the imposing weight of a colonial past or the seductive prospect of the sort of progress promoted by Europe and America as if it were the only possibility for national fulfilment. El-Wakil and Badran now have their counterparts in every other country and religious culture in the developing world and each of these freely acknowledge the huge debt they owe to Fathy, who was the first to stand up against this overwhelming force. The question of how these countries and belief systems will eventually address the issue of cultural, regional or religious identity that has not been answered, and the way that the question should be structured, is a hotly debated theoretical issue today, but the fact that it is being asked at all is directly attributable to Hassan Fathy. This is his most important and enduring legacy.

Chronology

Talka Primary School

Cairo 1928, *constructed*

The architect's first major project after graduation, and a testimony to the Beaux-Arts formality of his education at the University of Cairo, the Talka school is neo-classical in style, with engaged columns, pediments and acrotyrion executed in precise detail.

La Giardinara Kiosk

Bulaq 1930, *construction not verified*

Intended as an addition to a house in Bulaq, this Kiosk design shows ingenious utilization of existing walls, and efficient use of space.

Husni Omar Villa

Giza 1930, *construction not verified*

The Husni Omar house is starkly modern in style, with flat roofs, white stucco walls, and severe, steel industrial windows. Designed in conjunction with Ahmad Omar, who was related to the client, the villa represents the first of several International Style designs completed at this time.

Sada al-Bariya Villa

1930, *construction not verified*

Designed for Fumm al-Khalig in Egypt, the Sada al-Bariya Villa pragmatically links living quarters for the owner with two additional rental units. All three elements, while joined, are self-contained with separate internal stairs making a two-storey plan feasible. While the building again reflects a Modernist direction, there is a vestigial central court used to provide privacy, and evidence of the kind of spatial organization that was to become so characteristic of the architect's work.

Bosphore Casino

Cairo 1932, *construction not verified*

Intended to be located on the corner of the old Queen Nazli Boulevard at Bab al-Hadid, in Cairo, the Bosphore Casino is another of the architect's incongruously Modernist early works. Designed for the Qudsi brothers, the art deco-style structure, however, shows confident handling of a difficult curved corner site, and authoritative use of massing.

Al-Kachkacin Printing Shop

Cairo 1933, *construction not verified*

Designed for Mustafa-Bey al-Kachkacin to expand his newspaper operation, this six-storey office building was to be the home of his *Abu al-Hol* and *al-Sabah Journal*, on al-Dakhliya Street in Cairo. Similar in style to the Omar and al-Bariya villas, with flat roof and industrial windows, it uses the grid and curtain-wall system then being put forward as part of the 'five points of architecture' in Europe.

Azmi Bey Abd al-Malik Villa

Cairo 1934, *construction not verified*

Similar to the al-Beyli villa in style, but rectangular, rather than square in plan, using a Western-style distribution of rooms around a central entry hall on the ground floor. In elevation, flat white stucco walls surmount a brick dado interspersed with planters. Decorative cast-iron grillework relieves severe, rectilinear windows.

Al-Beyli Villa

Cairo 1934, *construction not verified*

On a restricted lot only about eighteen metres square, this small house for Abd al-Halim Bey al-Beyli makes best use of its tight boundaries by

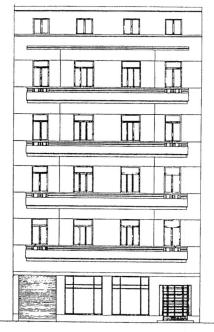

Al-Kachkacin Printing Shop, elevation

deferring to both the northern and western property lines, to allow more open space on the other two sides of the house. Like other buildings of Fathy's early period, it is Modernist in style.

Madkur Housing and Shops

Cairo 1934, *construction not verified*

Little documentary evidence of this design remains, but the drawings that do exist show a multi-storey building that was meant to have been built for Hasan Pasha Madkur in the Muski district of Cairo, with commercial shops on the ground floor and offices and apartments distributed over two floors above.

Garvice Villa

1937, *construction not verified*

In marked divergence from the nine projects that precede it chronologically, this house, for Mrs Isabel Garvice, utilizes several new elements, such as a central courtyard, separation of public and private spaces, *maqa'ad*, and *mashrabiya* screens set in otherwise blank exterior walls. Named 'Dar al-Islam', or the world of Islam, the villa provides a turning point in the architect's development; but the new direction that it indicates has yet to become convincingly integral to his architecture and at best represents a tentative point of transition.

Taher al-Omari Bey Villa

Fayyum 1937, *construction not verified*

This villa (often listed as 'Bek', a misreading of the honorific 'Bey') was intended for a site in Sidmant al-Gabal in the Fayyum, and exhibits more dramatic evidence of a change in Fathy's philosophy toward a more localized architecture. The long, linear plan is characterized by a *malkaf* and *qa'a* facing out into a walled formal garden, at the centre of the house.

Al-Harini Villa

Giza 1938, *construction not verified*

Built one year after the Garvice Villa and the resthouse for Taher al-Omari, this house for Mrs al-Harini in Giza shows the extent to which Fathy was still searching for direction at this critical point in his career and was still attracted by fashionable Western values. He briefly reverts to the International Style once again here, using a high cylindrical glass stair enclosure to dominate the front of an Adolf Loos-like elevation. Several major gestures, however, such as the use of a hidden inner garden, which is protected from the street by an arched screen wall, hint at things to come.

Fathy Villa

1938, *construction not verified*

Sited in Kom al-Akhdar, this villa was designed for Fathy's brother Muhammad, who went on to become a well known composer of songs based on classical Arabian themes.

While conventionally organized in plan, with an entry foyer and central stairwell giving access into a formal living room and dining room arrangement, the exterior of the house utilizes a strong Mediterranean theme, with vertical forms capped with red-tiled roofs predominating.

Hayat Villa

Cairo 1938, *construction not verified*

The drawings for this compact residence, intended for the Dokki area of Cairo, are headed 'Pour le célèbre artiste Hayat Muhammad' ('for the famous artist Hayat Muhammad') and are also signed by Ahmad Omar, who collaborated on the Husni Omar Villa of 1930. His continued influence here may explain the similarity in style between the two houses.

Hishmat Villa

Cairo 1938, *construction not verified*

This was to be a stately mansion located in Dokki, for Zaynab Hanem Hishmat.

Badran Villa

1940, *construction not verified*

Partially executed drawings indicate intentions for a two-storey residence, with a highly formalized and colonnaded central entrance hall, to be built in brick.

Al-Bakliya resthouse

Kafr al-Hima 1940, *construction not verified*

This remodelling of a resthouse for M. E. G. Takla Pasha was for his farm on an agricultural road in Kafr al-Hima, and was intended as an adjunct for a large villa already built within a walled compound. Watercolour renderings of this project that have survived indicate the importance that the architect placed upon its presentation to the client.

Rural Farms

Egypt 1940–41, *constructed*

Using what he jokingly called his 'itinerant band of masons', Fathy travelled to various farming villages such as Mit al-Nasara, testing his new-found structural system in the building of several groups of shelters. While largely utilitarian in nature, these projects were to provide him with the confidence he needed to use the Nubian vault and dome system much more extensively at New Gourna five years later.

Rural Hospitals

Egypt 1940–41, *construction not verified*

Several hospital projects were designed for various villages throughout Egypt using the Nubian construction techniques that Fathy had discovered in Upper Egypt. They were a revelation to him, allowing him to build the spatial system he had begun to develop from 1937 onwards in mud brick, without costly wooden supports.

Al-Razik Villa

Abu Girg 1941, *construction not verified*

One of two houses designed for the al-Razik family, this first residence (for Isma'il Abd al-Razik) shows evidence of several stages of evolution before arriving at a final, balanced scheme. In its last form, the architect set up a strong sequence of formal reception spaces, related to the public function of hospitality to guests, along a north–south axis. In contrast to this, he designed all the private, family spaces along a counter-axis, and the intersection of each of these elements forms a series of external courtyards that relate to each grouping. An evocative gouache of this house, perhaps one of the best the architect ever completed, clearly proclaims a firmly established set of values, with all elements of his architectural vocabulary fully in command and integral to his principles.

Farid-Bey Villa

1941, *construction not verified*

Although completed in the same prolific year that produced the Royal Society of Agriculture Farm, Izbit al-Basri prototype house and al-Razik Villa, the house for Husayn Bey Farid surprisingly lacks the virtuosity displayed elsewhere. Flat roofs are used instead of domes and vaults, and pointed arcades replace regular arches.

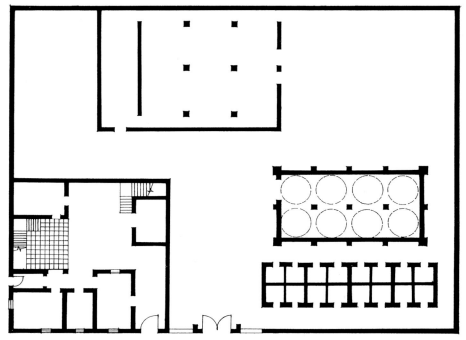

Royal Society of Agriculture Farm, plan

Royal Society of Agriculture Farm

Bahtim 1941, *constructed*

This project was cited by Fathy in *Architecture for the Poor* at the beginning of his search for alternative methods of constructing roofs, the most expensive part of a house at this time. Wartime material shortages imposed strict limits on cost; an inexpensive standard method was needed. The prototypes he developed here first failed, prompting Fathy to learn about traditional Nubian building techniques. After an important visit to Nubian villages at Aswan, he returned with several masons to finish the project.

The complex consisted of housing, a stable for cattle (both with flat roofs), high-domed granaries and a pigeon-cote, all organized within a single boundary wall with one main gate.

Takla Pasha Resthouse

Kafr al–Hima 1941, *construction not verified*

This was a large resthouse with several alternative plans that each show the development of a central, formal *qa'a*, or reception area, possibly related to those for the al-Bakliya Farm done for the same client two years earlier.

Chilean Nitrate Company Resthouse

Safaga 1942, *construction not verified*

As a headquarters for a company based in Safaga, just south of the resort city of Hurghada on the Red Sea Coast, this building grew from a modest staff shelter to become four spacious units separated by massive party-walls, sharing a single lounge and dining facility. Each of the living units has a large domed living room with fireplace, bedroom, bath and outdoor patio overlooking the Red Sea.

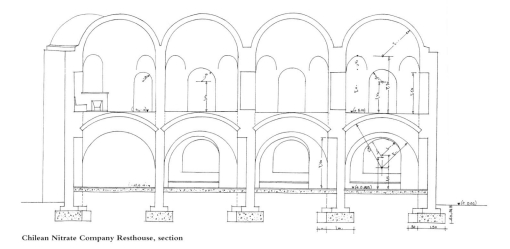

Chilean Nitrate Company Resthouse, section

Hamed Said House

Marg 1942, *constructed; extended* **1945**

Built in two phases, the Hamed Said house began with a large vaulted loggia, which was used as an entry and as a sitting area from which to view what was once lush green countryside, and a domed studio space with an attached *iwan* for sleeping. A second phase, built three years later, added a dining room, kitchen and bathing wing, which is linked by an articulated gallery to a larger studio across a central court.

The house is notable for what Hamed Said has called 'achieving the maximum result with the minimum means', as well as the ease with which the two phases are joined. Two mature trees were incorporated into the central courtyard, and dictated its size. This court has now become the focal point of the weekly meetings of the 'Society of Art and Life', held by Hamed Said and his wife.

Prototype House

Izbit al–Basri 1942, *constructed*

This small house, which was built beside a canal between Cairo and Maadi, was intended to prove to the Red Crescent Society that it could serve as an economical model to replace twenty-five houses that had been destroyed by flood shortly before.

The house, built in only forty days, contained a guest reception room, or *qa'a*, dining area and kitchen, and a large sleeping area, which were all domed and grouped around a *maqa'ad* in the court. Features such as an entry offset for privacy, decorative claustra-work ventilation and

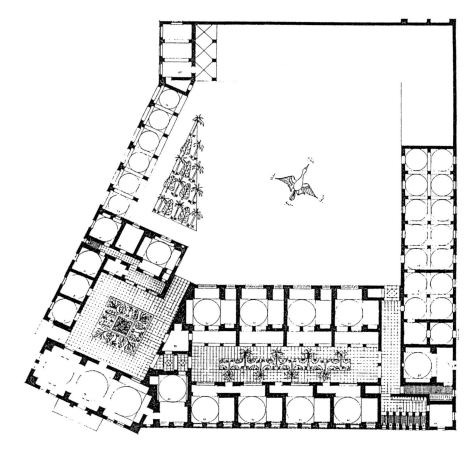

School at New Gourna, plan

square central court; in the final building the courtyard was moved to the exterior, serving as a raised platform from which to take advantage of the magnificent views. The house is built on timber framing with a single mud-brick dome over the *qa'a*; the flat part of the roof is used as a sleeping area. The villa is located on the tip of a promontory on the Birkit Qarun, permitting unrestricted views of the lake on three sides.

Kallini House

Menia 1945, *construction not verified*

Several similarities between the plan of this villa and that of the preliminary design for the Nasr House, which preceded it, indicate that the architect may have determined to recycle the rejected, earlier scheme. In the process however, the architect reworked certain parts of the plan, such as the public entry sequence and family area, to make this one of the best-resolved designs of his career. Like the first Nasr house scheme, this also has an accentuated sense of vertical scale.

Hassanein Mausoleum

Cairo 1946, *constructed*

Commissioned by a grateful government as a memorial to a respected advisor, this mausoleum still stands alongside Salah Salem Street at the outer fringe of the 'City of the Dead' outside Cairo. Fathy, who was Ahmad Hassanein's brother-in-law, followed the intent of that commission and designed it in the style of the Mamluk mausoleums between the twelfth and fifteenth centuries, adding a delicate, double-gated garden as a forecourt that has unfortunately not remained intact.

coloured glass *umriyad* stars in the domes gave the houses a distinctive character and dignity. Expecting to win the commission with ease on the basis of spaciousness and low cost, Fathy was shocked to be passed over in favour of a more expensive concrete prototype; his unit was demolished. He describes the history of this project in *Architecture for the Poor*.

Abd al-Razik Villa

Bani Mazar 1943, *construction not verified*

Extensive drawings of this villa, which was the second done for the al-Razik family (in this case for Hasan), show a much larger scheme than had been attempted earlier.

Said al-Bakri Villa

Zamalek 1943, *construction not verified*

Intended for a site in Zamalek, then far more rural than it is today, this villa demonstrates careful articulation of spaces, and further development of the idea of the sanctity of family privacy, which was to be a vital part of all Fathy's residential work from this point forward.

Hamdi Seif al-Nasr House

Fayyum 1945, *constructed*

Built for an influential landowner, who was also the Minister of War at that time, this villa underwent radical changes between the preliminary design and final construction. Despite the reduction in scale of the final building from the first plans, many of the spatial relationships of the original scheme were retained. The plan is organized around a large

New Gourna Village

Luxor 1946, *partially constructed*

Undoubtedly Hassan Fathy's best-known project because of the popularity of his book *Architecture for the Poor* which details its history, New Gourna Village was commissioned by the Egyptian Department of Antiquities to solve the problem of tomb-robbing in the Valley of the Kings, Queens and Nobles nearby.

In seeking to relocate the five contiguous villages of Old Gourna on the slopes near the valley, which relate to the five separate tribes that occupied them, Fathy devised a village plan based on equivalent *badanas*, or tribal neighbourhoods, and sought to provide the Gournii with an entirely new economy, based on agriculture and sales of traditional crafts to tourists, rather than illicit archaeology. The plan was based on the principle of what city planner Jacqueline Tyrwhitt, who was later to work with Fathy at the Ekistics Centre in Athens, was aptly to call the 'human scale intermediary'. In practice, this concept utilized courtyards of various sizes, from a large public square, to intermediate neighbourhood plazas, and finally small, internal residential courts, to act as architectural decompression valves for residents and visitors alike; to delineate public and private areas and prevent the anonymity so endemic in other housing projects attempted at this time.

Fathy also took the unheard-of step of personalizing the housing here, rather than replicating a similar unit, in order to make the Village more humane. As he said, 'In Nature no two men are alike. Even if they are twins and physically identical, they will differ in their dreams. The architecture of the house emerges from the dream. This is why, in villages built by their inhabitants, we will find no two houses identical.'

In spite of his customized approach, he did intend this project to be a prototype for others to follow, both in planning principles and method of construction, in order finally to provide an economical solution to the problem of housing Egypt's poor.

Construction proceeded from the large central square outwards, and public buildings such as the mosque, *khan*, theatre, town hall, exhibition centre, market and boys' school, along with the house that the architect used as a working site office and private residence, were completed first. The mosque has been well maintained.

Due to obstacles so graphically described in the architect's own detailed account of the project, work was stopped with only one-fifth of the Village having been completed. Yet it was such a radical and refreshingly uncomplicated departure from other failed attempts at public housing in both the developing and industrialized world since, that it has served as a model for all 'self-help' communities to follow. New Gourna still has enormous influence on all those contemplating similar projects.

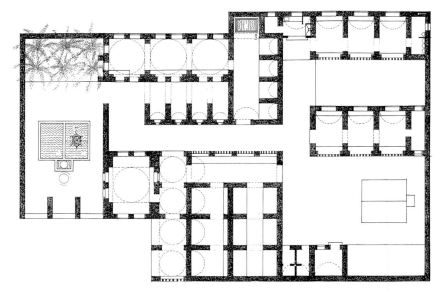

Ceramics Factory, Garagus, plan

Tusun Abu Gabal House

1947, *constructed*

While similar to both the Taher al-Omari Bey and Kallini houses in form, this house, near the Turkish Embassy along the Nile Corniche in Giza, has been built in concrete. Given the architect's dislike of that material, the decision to do so was probably made against his wishes.

Eid House

Zagazig 1948, *construction not verified*

Three different plans have survived of this house, which was designed for Mrs Raymond Eid for her farm near Zagazig. While decidedly different in character, each shows a plan form that spirals out from a central *qa'a*, forming three separate external courtyards which are individually protected by the projecting wings. The roof in each case varies, being flat in one version, domed in the other two. This exercize, like many others in the architect's *œuvre*, shows the surprising amount of design development that characterized his work.

Villa for Aziza Hanem Hassanein

1949, *constructed*

This house, which Fathy designed for his wife on a beautiful site next to the Nile, between

Cairo and Maadi, had to be demolished in 1951 due to the widening of a road nearby. Another small residence that he designed for her, and which was built in Maadi itself near the present metro station, has been radically altered, and is now virtually unrecognizable. The first villa on the Nile Corniche was built in white limestone to an exquisite level of finish, with various intricate patterns of floor tiles, and many finely worked *mashrabiya* screens. All were lost in the course of demolition.

Ceramics Factory, Garagus

1950, *constructed*

This pottery and ceramic production facility was initiated by the Jesuit Mission to assist the economy of a small farming village in Upper Egypt. The director of this mission had been impressed by both the low cost and style of New Gourna and approached Fathy for assistance in the planning of this workshop. While hardly a 'factory' in the typical sense, the workshop, as designed by the architect, accurately and efficiently records the process of ceramic making in a long, linear plan, from the delivery of the raw earth, through turning, firing, glazing and sale. As was the case in so many of the architect's realized projects, however, major changes to his design were made during construction that turned the project into something quite different.

Cultural Centre, Garagus

1950, *construction not verified*

At the same time as he designed the Garagus ceramic production facility, Fathy also provided the Jesuit mission in Egypt with plans for a Cultural and Health Centre for this small village in Qena Province, made up of a church, crafts school, and clinic. Each of these three elements in turn are grouped in individual clusters around an open court, and linked by a wall that is provided with a main gate and side gate for access into the compound. The church is grouped with the church school area, and an assembly room, while the crafts school on the opposite side of the court consists mainly of classrooms for teaching weaving, and a large workshop. Rounded walls and curved forms predominate in this unusual scheme.

Lulu'at al-Sahara

near Cairo 1950, *constructed*

As an addition to a plantation owned by Hafiz Afifi-Pasha, this small village, whose name means 'The Pearl of the Sahara', was provided as a social service by the landlord to his large staff. To existing housing, health services facilities, workshops, and farm buildings that had all been built by the owner ten years earlier, Fathy added six additional housing units and a small mosque and *madrasa*. The housing that he provided is unique in that it consists of tandem two-storey dwellings that are separated by an offset *magaz*, or passage at the base, but linked with patios staggered for family privacy, above. The mosque is a small jewel and is meticulously maintained by the community of workers.

Monastirli House

Cairo 1950, *constructed*

At first glance, this villa by the Nile may seem to recall the stylistic direction of the architect's work during the transitional period of 1937 to 1940, in such projects as the Villas Hayat and Heshmat, and yet, upon closer inspection, the house is more complex. The strong personality of the client, Mrs Atiya Monastirli, wife of the then Egyptian Ambassador to Turkey, clearly emerges here, but Fathy's signature is equally evident. The siting of the house, for example, manages to make the most of an oddly shaped, triangular piece of land by placing utilitarian functions at a right angle to the main body of the house, along the base of the triangle, in order to create a feeling of enclosure in the entry court. The house itself gradually expands towards a large sitting room that is cantilevered out over the river and uses corner windows to make the most of the morning and evening views of the Nile. The entry sequence into the house, for guests, is also carefully controlled, bringing them away from the private zone in stepped sequence toward a formal reception space, covered with an elegant ornate plasterwork dome. The spaces related to guests, which are obviously very important to a diplomat and his wife, are equally graced with views of the river, but are set back from the shore in order to allow those views to be filtered through the palm trees in a garden outside. Such personal touches continue, culminating in an upper internal court that uses the apex of the plaster dome directly below as a fountainhead, and mirrors it in an open lattice pergola of extraordinary delicacy above.

Atiya Monastirli was especially fond of the residential architecture along the Bosphorus in Istanbul, and encouraged Fathy to visit there for an extended period to study it. This visit, which also meant a great deal to him because of his own Turkish background on his maternal side, undoubtedly influenced the design, as did several Ottoman palaces in Cairo, such as the extensive harem of the palace of Muhammad Ali on the Citadel which has since been demolished.

Mosque

Punjab, India 1950, *construction not verified*

Both *baratsi* trusses in concrete and geodesic domes are used in this mosque. Aside from these unconventional elements of his design, Fathy went on to work out a scheme for an inexpensive house as a part of this exercize, which also uses folded slabs in the *baratsi* format in conjunction with a large wind catch.

Stopplaere House

Luxor 1950, *constructed*

This project was built for Dr Alexander Stopplaere, then the chief restorer for the Department of Antiquities, who had admired Fathy's work at New Gourna. Having been asked to provide quarters for Dr Stopplaere, as well as for staff who would be assisting him during the archaeological season at Luxor, the architect began with the idea of a central courtyard totally surrounded by the working and living spaces required by the programme; these were arranged in a square around it. Eventually, the prerequisites of the location, on a high ridge alongside the main road into the Valley of the Kings and Queens, began to open up the square into a rectilinear form, in which Dr Stopplaere's quarters fell naturally into place on one side of the middle court, and the staff quarters occupied the other. A long gallery, similar to the one that had successfully served to join the two halves of the Hamed Said house earlier, re-emerges here to solve a similar problem, with equally effective results. Smaller courtyards are also introduced in other areas of the house to bring in light, and yet retain privacy.

Zaki Villa

Helwan 1951, *construction not verified*

This small villa for artist Shaaban Zaki was to be located on Isma'il Pasha Kamel Street in Helwan. Early studies indicate modest plans for a two-storey house with a large painting studio on the ground floor, and other social spaces grouped around an arcaded garden and pool.

Tile Factory

Jerusalem 1952, *construction not verified*

A rather utilitarian structure, specified for construction in the 'Dome of the Rock' area, perhaps intended for making the tiles to be used in the restoration of that important Islamic monument.

Alexandria Resthouse

Aswan 1955, *construction not verified*

Located to the southwest of Jabal Tagug, near Aswan, on a steep, curving escarpment, this house has one of the most animated and unusual of any of Fathy's plans. Existing in rough sketches only, the location is tantalizingly close to the cliff face, matching the topographical contours to a remarkable extent.

Muhammad Musa Villa

Imbaba 1955, *construction not verified*

This small, two-storey dwelling was planned for the Munira area, in Imbaba, Egypt.

Harraniya Weaving Village

1957, *designed, but not constructed*

Prepared as a proposal for his close friend Ramsis Wissa Wassif, this complex plan includes weavers' workshops, commercial areas, housing units and agricultural fields, combined into one self-sufficient venture, on land already owned by the Wissa Wassif family in Shabramant near Cairo.

According to Ramsis' sister, Ceres, the ideas proposed were too extensive for the activities envisioned by the family at that time, and a more modest experiment was begun. Having been expanded incrementally over the years, the Ramsis Wissa Wassif Centre is now world-renowned for the beautiful tapestries created by its young weavers, using wool and natural vegetable dyes produced on site.

Schools

Fares and Idfu 1957, *constructed*

The Fares school, which was designed for the Egyptian Ministry of Education for a small village between Luxor and Aswan in Upper Egypt, was intended to be a low-cost prototype to be used in other rural areas of the country, where illiteracy rates were alarmingly high. Consisting of ten classrooms, a library, assembly hall, craft rooms, administrative offices and a mosque with ablution facilities, the school is organized around space that also serves as a playground for the children during recess. About 700 students, divided almost evenly between boys and girls, attend the school which is the only one in the village. While the classrooms were originally intended to be naturally cooled by a *malkaf-salsabil* combination, the *salsabil* was finally not included for reasons of space. In spite of the omission of these water fountains, each classroom is very cool on the hottest days of early summer. Roofing of the classrooms, which was meant to enhance the difference between the teaching area, which was domed, and the *malkaf-salsabil* location, which was vaulted, was carried out as the architect intended, in spite of the internal modifications.

Another school, built to the same prototype, was constructed in Idfu, nearby, but has not been well maintained, and is now near collapse.

Arab Refugee Housing

1957, *prototype, implementation not verified*

This design for a prototype for temporary housing for Palestinian refugees actually proposes three types of unit, all organized on a five-metre-square module, with four units meant to be grouped together on the foundation base. The use of a module here adds a great deal of flexibility to a bearing wall system, which is often dismissed as being too static for such construction.

Iraq Housing Project

1958, *construction not verified*

As a member of the Doxiades Organization in Athens between 1957 and 1962, Fathy entered wholeheartedly into both the intellectual and social activities of the Ekistics group, lecturing on the relationship between climate and architecture at Athens Technical Institute and joining the 'City of the Future' research project then underway at the Ekistics Centre itself.

The drawings for the Iraq Housing Program, which were associated with this project, include master planning of an entire city, as well as a detailed examination of one component. This component, representing one neighbourhood in the city, is made up of all the elements of a traditional Iraqi village, such as a mosque, market shops, coffee-house, school and houses, with the addition of a park and *immaret*, or administration centre. Closer examination of the drawings for what he called Hussiyah Village, while initially giving pause because of an occasional lapse into 'beton brut', which is used as a gesture toward his patron, show a deep concern for the separation of pedestrian and vehicular circulation, and for the types of housing provided for different classes of people, including farming and non-farming families as well as government officials, and tradesmen. The drawings are also accompanied by sketches of vernacular houses with stone basements designed to trap cool night air for recirculation through the house during hot summer days, indicating that they be used as models for single-family houses, with the old system incorporated into the new designs.

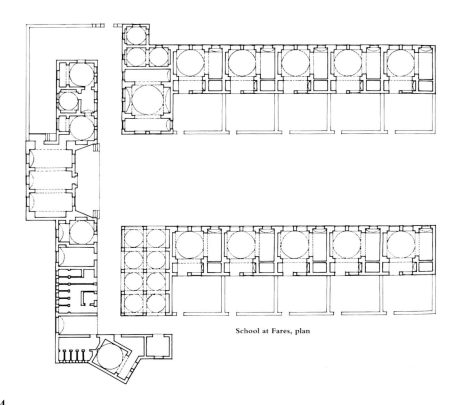

School at Fares, plan

Baume-Marpent Resthouse

1959, *construction not verified*

Staff quarters for the Baume-Marpent Enterprise at the Kharga Oasis, consisting of three large dormitory-style sleeping areas, meeting rooms, and a grand reception room with wind catch and water-cooling *salsabil* in the corner. The arcaded meeting rooms look out onto flanking walled gardens on each side as linear transition elements between the public reception area and the private staff quarters.

Ali Bey Fathy Apartment

1960, *construction not verified*

Adapted from a previous design, the plan for this apartment for Fathy's brother works within a curved exterior glass curtain wall, taking advantage of the view, and uses a projecting *baratsi* truss roof to shade the glass. As in the Mehrez apartment, extremely efficient use of limited space characterizes the design, which also takes advantage of the exterior roof-top area for outside pergola-covered patios.

Atiya Restaurant

1960, *construction not verified*

The elevation of this long, linear building, for an unspecified site, is dominated by two high *malkafs*, which combine with inner courtyards at each end of the restaurant, to cool it. Seating within is distributed evenly between tables, banquettes and long counters, with a central kitchen serving all three.

Maaruf Muhammad Maaruf Housing

Cairo 1960, *construction not verified*

A three-storey apartment building for Maaruf Muhammad Maaruf and Muhammad Saad, who were acting as partners in the venture, to be located in the Khalifa district in Cairo. A large, projecting *mashrabiya* bay, similar to that used in the medieval al-Sinnari house in Old Cairo, turns what might otherwise be considered a rather conventional apartment layout into a memorable and commercially attractive design.

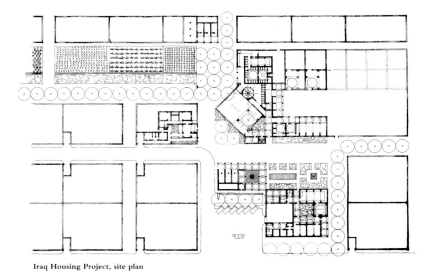

Iraq Housing Project, site plan

Touheimi Stables

1960, *construction not verified*

Various untitled sketches of plans by Fathy end with a finely drafted version showing twenty square, domed stalls constructed in mud brick surrounding a rectilinear stable yard, with office space, tack rooms and feed areas attached at one side, with their own internal open space. As is consistently the case in Fathy's work, compositional skill and a uniform structural language combine to lift what is usually considered to be a very utilitarian building type to a new, and much higher level of regard.

Villa for the Ambassador for Nigeria

Niamey, Nigeria 1960, *construction not verified*

To be located in Niamey, Nigeria, this villa responds to the intense heat of the area by carefully balancing inside and outside space so that natural ventilation can benefit all parts of the house. Utilizing the principles of the *takhtabush* Fathy always manages to align each exposed wing of the residence between courtyards, and to ensure that only one of these courtyards is planted, to generate maximum air flow from a cooler, landscaped area to a hotter, paved area.

High Institute for Popular Arts

Aswan 1962, *designed*

This Institute, commissioned by the Ministry of Culture, was intended to foster a deeper awareness of Egyptian history, particularly as revealed in folk art. To be located near the Nubian settlement of Abu al-Riche, on the outskirts of Aswan, the project was to be composed of a museum as well as various theatres, a school of dance, and an exhibition area in which various types of buildings from the past were to become a permanent lesson in Egyptian architectural history.

The museum segment of the Institute was designed as a succession of four increasingly higher *qa'as*, which each replicated those from the most historically important houses in medieval Cairo. This was done both to inform the public of an endangered legacy, and to preserve and maintain that legacy within a more manageable environment.

Shri Zahir Ahmed Villa

Hyderabad, India 1963, *construction not verified*

Designed for a site in Pangutta near Hyderabad, this small villa is an obvious exception to the architectural language that Fathy had developed by this point, but does incorporate air-cooling techniques similar to those used in the house of the Ambassador for Nigeria three years earlier.

Carr House

Liodessi, Greece 1964, *designed but not built*

Several proposals for a country house for Marion Carr, who wanted to build a retreat in Liodessi, near Athens, show Fathy's exploration of local

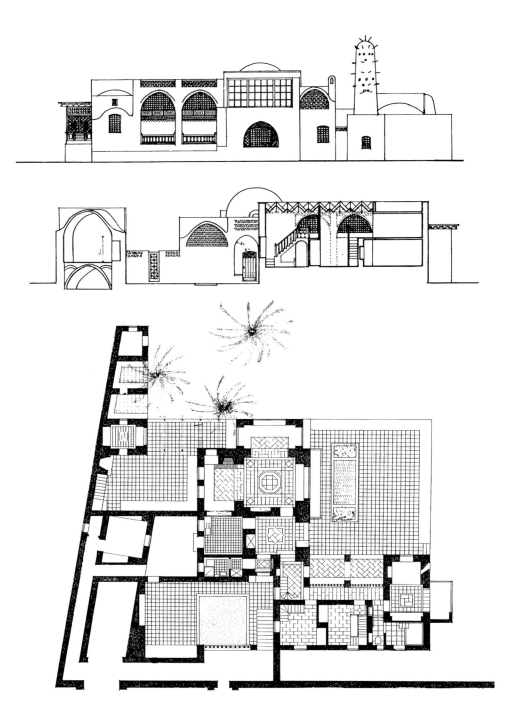

Fouad Riad House, elevation (top), section and plan

vernacular construction methods, especially in roofing. The linear form of the house, however, remains constant throughout, with rooms arranged in series along a gallery to take advantage of the view of nearby olive groves.

Roshdi Said House

Maadi 1965, *construction not verified*

This residence on a lot on Street 12 in Maadi is notable in several respects, not the least of which is a studious attempt by the architect to continue to use domed and vaulted roof forms, but to play them down on the exterior in favour of more rectilinear elements. Given the rather conservative architectural character of the area concerned, this may have been done in deference to the client's request, as the partial screening and concealment of all curved lines in the elevation certainly appears to be intentional.

The second notable detail is the use of relieving arches to carry a second floor, a technique which Fathy first observed at the Deir al-Samaan (St Simeon Monastery) in Aswan, built between the seventh and tenth centuries AD. Similar arches are used in the refectory there, to carry the floor of the monks' dormitory above.

Thirdly, the Said house uses *baratsi* trusses extensively, and is one of the architect's rare projects in Egypt to do so.

Fouad Riad House

Shabramant 1967, *constructed*

Fathy deals with difficult site conditions here with his usual, seemingly effortless mastery, turning the back of the house to the road which runs past it, engaging the thick boundary wall. With a canal and a mature stand of palm trees as limiting factors, inner space usage is closely defined. In contrast to the solid, protective entry, the front of the house opens onto a breathtaking view of the Pyramids of Giza in the distance. Built in unplastered stone rather than mud-brick, the house is highly complex.

Shahira Mehrez Apartment

Cairo 1967, *constructed*

This renovation of the sixth floor of an apartment building in Dokki presented the architect with a very difficult challenge, as he had to work within an awkwardly placed arrangement of pre-existing concrete columns, beams and stairs.

That challenge, however, has been ingeniously met, providing a sophisticated and surprisingly spacious *pied-à-terre*, from which the client could pursue her growing commercial interests involving traditional crafts. Using the stairway and elevator as a point of demarcation, Fathy placed the shop and office to the left of the stair landing, and the apartment itself to the right, to be reached through an inconspicuous, indirect hallway, which is treated like a *magaz*, for privacy. Once inside the apartment an entirely different world is revealed, with a central *qa'a*, capped with a finely detailed wooden *shukshaykha*, dominating the entire arrangement. This gives the feeling of being in medieval Cairo instead of at the top of a block of flats in the middle of one of the most crowded parts of the city. This *qa'a* is augmented by another comfortable and more private sitting room, organized around a fireplace, as well as an outdoor patio that serves as the exterior component of the sitting room, to be used on hot summer evenings.

The apartment is a virtuoso performance in architectural scale, proportion, level and detail.

New Baris Village

Kharga 1967, *partially constructed*

No other project dominates this mature phase of the architect's work as much as the village of New Baris. It is comparable to New Gourna twenty years before, Fathy's best-known community project.

Discovery of a large water well sixty kilometres south of the Kharga Oasis in 1963, which had been estimated to have the capacity continuously to irrigate up to 1000 acres of land, led the Organization for Desert Development to propose an agricultural community. This remote outpost in a forbidding wilderness, almost in the geographical centre of Egypt, was initially planned to house 250 families, of which more than half were intended to be farmers and the remainder to be service personnel. His previous experience with such a project, and ability to build it inexpensively, made Fathy the logical choice as the architect for New Baris. The potential occupants of New Baris were a totally unknown quantity. Fathy himself describes it:

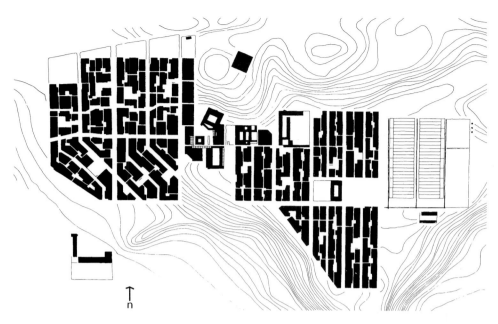

Baris was an interesting problem in which I was to create all the parts of a community, to bring together in the best manner possible people whom I did not know. All that I had at my disposal were demographic, geographic and climatic surveys. I had to provide the aesthetics, the sense of man in a space constructed by man.

Fathy made a thorough study of both the traditional architecture and climate of the region. In addition to examining the fourth century AD mud-brick ruins of the necropolis of Bagawat nearby, he also closely observed the existing village of Kharga, where the material used, as well as the width and orientation of the streets and introverted forms of the houses, effectively offset summer temperatures as high as 50 degrees centigrade. These considerations, along with the additional need for the cold storage of the fruits and vegetables grown by the community prior to shipping, and the impossibility of providing air-conditioning, led Fathy to focus on natural systems as the formative influence on the new village. By putting the storage areas below grade and refining the *malkaf* designs he had used previously by adding baffles, incrementally reduced air-shafts and secondary towers to accelerate circulation, temperature reductions of up to 15 degrees centigrade were achieved. The *suq*, or market place, became the active heart of a community which spirals out to fit a steeply graded ridge on either side of it. This *suq*,

and other communal buildings around it, differ from their predecessors at New Gourna both in the practical functions represented and the compactness of the open spaces between the buildings themselves. Construction was stopped in 1967 by war, and sadly was never resumed. But Fathy's success in overcoming potentially insurmountable obstacles with previously untested natural methods, as well as the powerful visual impression made by the resulting forms, make Baris a tectonic lesson for architects today.

Social Centre

Bulaq 1968, *construction not verified*

Like the Ali Bey Fathy apartment, this is another rare example of the architect's uncharacteristic use of curved plan forms, but the reason here is not as clear. Phasing diagrams indicate plans for future expansion on top of an initial structure housing clothing workshops and a sales room, as well as administrative offices, for community-produced goods.

Khoronfesh Nursery

1969, *construction not verified*

A small project, for an unknown location, using a central, drum-like *qa'a*, with flat-roofed wings flanking it on either side, providing an entirely open rectilinear floor area for the care of children. The *qa'a* is cut in two by another floor above, which increases available floor area, but uncharacteristically restricts the feeling of vertical space that the architect achieves elsewhere in the use of this traditional form.

Abu al-Qichr' Laboratory

1970, *construction not verified*

A laboratory for homeopathic medicine in an unknown location provides work and office space in a two-part complex, joined by party-wall, of which each has its own central court. The client was Dr Ibrahim Abu al-Qichr'.

IFAO field house

1970, *construction not verified*

This six-unit staff quarters for the Institut Français de l'Archéologie Orientale in Cairo, was probably intended for operations in Luxor, although this has yet to be confirmed. Each unit consists of a domed central *qa'a*, with two flanking *iwans* for sleeping, and an ensuite bath, all of which are cooled by a wind catch. The arrangement of *iwans* indicates that each unit would be shared by two people, and the projection of one of the six units forward, giving it more prominence, suggests that it may have been intended for the director.

Jeddah Duplex Housing

1970, *construction not verified*

This was to be a housing block of rather straightforward plan, consisting of three different kinds of unit, distributed over two separate floors each enclosing a large, central court.

Co-operative Centre

Kharga 1970, *constructed*

This project, commissioned by the Desert Development and Reclamation Bureau, was seen as a key part of governmental plans to found a series of new towns around the Kharga Oasis, using the substantial amount of water available in the aquifer there for the establishment of agricultural villages. This Centre provides the back-up facilities necessary for those villages,

since many of the intended residents would not necessarily have had any previous background in farming. Technical and educational services assist residents in planting, soil productivity and machinery maintenance. The Centre itself has suffered from lack of the perennial plastering needed to protect the mud-brick walls, as well as from heaving and swelling of the soil, caused by broken water mains. Rather than correcting these problems, the administrators at the Centre have been replacing collapsing structures with reinforced concrete units.

Luxor Cultural Centre

1970, *partially constructed*

Designed for the Ministry of Culture, this centre was intended to be located in the heart of the town of Luxor itself near the Fatimid Mosque of Sidi al-Wahsh, and the park that is adjacent to it. Only the main hall of the large complex has been completed, however, but the architect's intentions for natural ventilation have been ignored. A large *malkaf* that was intended to cool the entire inside area has been built, but closed off, rendering the entire roof form meaningless.

New Gourna Touristic Village

1970, *designed*

The tragedy of New Gourna was not over for Fathy with the end of construction in 1948, but continued through attempts to revive the moribund project, and to counter the reluctance of the Gournii to move there because of their wish to remain close to the tombs in the Valley of the Kings. The addition of a touristic village, to be built to the west of the existing village, was felt to be the best way to accomplish this revival. Extensive plans organized around a diagonal street leading outward through a large gate, which was linked to the administration centre on the existing main square, included, among other amenities, an Egyptian centre for the development of creative crafts, shops and guest bungalows.

Priest's House

Garagus 1970, *construction not verified*

In addition to the Ceramic Factory and Cultural Centre at Garagus, this house was designed for a Jesuit priest at the village, nearly twenty years

after Fathy's original work there. The house is small, but makes full use of vertical space.

Prince Sadruddin Aga Khan House

Aswan 1970, *designed*

Sited near the tomb of the Aga Khan III in Aswan, on an island in the Nile, this small resthouse utilizes landscaping as well as a *takhtabush* at the end of a small garden to frame views toward the west bank of the river, and the sheer sand dunes coming down to it.

Princess Shahnaz Villa

1970, *construction not verified*

Little information survives about this villa, intended for a riverside site in Luxor, with arcaded gardens and pool near the Nile.

Siddiq Villa

1970, *construction not verified*

This villa and studio, designed for Rateb Siddiq, utilizes a repetitive three-vault module in different orientations around a domed *qa'a*.

Suq al-Silah

1970, *designed*

This recreation of a medieval *wikala*, designed for Suq al-Silah Street in Cairo, was divided into two projects, for Plot 45 and Plot 66. The larger of the two (Plot 45) uses the same configuration as the *wikalas* of the past, with a single massive doorway to give access into a long central court. The ground floor of each project is reserved for shops, and the upper levels for apartments.

Mosque and Conference Centre

Sudan 1970, *construction not verified*

Like the Mosque in Punjab, this project also uses a geodesic dome over the main prayer space, but the complex is more ambitious, with an assembly hall, office block and towering minaret encircling a large public open space.

Mosque

Tanta 1970, *construction not verified*

A hypostyle mosque design for Tanta, in the Delta region of Egypt, using extensive arcades to create a forecourt area of quite large scale and fine detail and intended as a part of the replanning of the al-Aref Billah Ahmad Badawi area of Tanta.

Mosque

Tripoli, Lebanon 1970, *construction not verified*

Only one plan of this mosque remains, showing the building itself, with its own imperative of orientation, placed at an angle between a *madrasa* to the south and a garden forecourt to the north.

Murad Ghaleb House

Cairo 1971, *construction not verified*

An elegant residence for the Pyramid area of Cairo, using a sinuous series of vaults to provide natural ventilation into an open swimming pool area that is the focal point of the house. These vaults are contained in the elevation by the terminal massing of the vertical, domed reception room at the main entrance, which completes the composition.

Nasser Mausoleum

Cairo 1971, *designed*

A monumental, vaguely Pharaonic, pylon gate is used as the main feature of this memorial to Egypt's late President Gamal Abd al-Nasser.

Architect's own house and Northern Shore Development

Sidi Krier 1971, *house constructed, development scheme designed*

The design for a development scheme was requested by the Planning Commission for the Development of Sidi Krier, on the Mediterranean shore of Egypt, after several members of the commission saw the architect's own house nearby. The development was to be a tourist resort facility, using stylistic features of Fathy's house.

The house itself is a delight, and a constant source of experimentation for the architect, who was always changing parts of it. The roof of the house is treated as an outside room, open to the sea air and view; a patio faces the water on the ground floor below. These features were revised over the course of time.

Polk House

Colorado, USA 1971, *construction not verified*

This house in the mountains of Aspen, Colorado, was designed for Dr William Polk who was most instrumental in the publication of Fathy's book *Architecture for the Poor* in America, and who also wrote the book's introduction. The house stretches out along a high ridge, overlooking groves of aspen trees.

Nassif House

Jeddah, Saudi Arabia 1973, *constructed*

The philosophical direction of this house, which would undoubtedly still draw comment in Saudi Arabia today, was especially novel in Jeddah in 1973, when the country and the city were caught up in the oil boom of that period, and the influence of International Style architecture that followed. Dr Abd al-Rahman Nassif's unwavering support of Fathy's ideas stemmed from his own conviction about the value of tradition, and they have now found much broader acceptance in a region that has seen much of its architectural heritage lost in the years since the house was built.

Sohar Remodelling

Oman 1974, *designed*

Fathy was asked by the Government of the Sultanate of Oman to replan the central business district of the port town of Sohar after its destruction by fire in 1967. For speed of construction he chose to use a modular system based on a 3.3-metre grid for each of the sixty new shops that he proposed. *Baratsi* truss roofs were selected for quick assembly and low cost. In addition to the shops, plans also included a market, mosque, administrative centre, and rural development housing with extensive gardens.

VIP House

Tabuk, Saudi Arabia 1974, *construction not verified*

This large-scale palace has two offset *qa'as* providing the core of the spatial organization. The completed set of working drawings for the project is detailed and extensive.

Wehda Mosque and Islamic Centre

Cairo 1974, *constructed, but not in accordance with the architect's plans*

Organized within an irregularly shaped site in the Abbasiya section of Cairo, this mosque is set upon a high podium base to separate it from the busy streets that surround it, and angles back to create an equally irregular arcaded court that is used as an entry, for additional privacy.

Dariya Housing

Saudi Arabia 1975, *one prototype built*

Fathy was commissioned by the United Nations Organization for Rural Development to design a prototypical housing unit for the village of Dariya while in Saudi Arabia during the programming stage of the Tabuk palace. The patriarchal home of the al-Saud family, Dariya interested him as a prime example of Najd mud-brick architecture in spite of the considerable damage done to the village over time. An excellent summary of the special character of this village can be found in 'The reconstruction of traditional structures in the al-Turayf Quarter of Dariya' by Michael Emrick and Carl Meinhardt, in the proceedings of the Sixth International Conference on the Conservation of Earthen Architecture, published by the Getty Conservation Institute. Fathy's own description is published in his article 'Model Houses for Dariya, Saudi Arabia', *Ekistics* issue 22, 1966.

Al-Mashrabiya Tourist Centre

Giza 1976, *designed*

Commissioned by the Shukri brothers for a busy street-side site in Giza, near the Pyramids, the plans were to include residential units, studios, restaurants, craft shops, a mosque and a theatre.

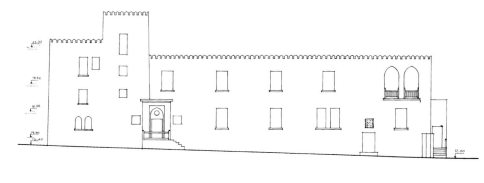

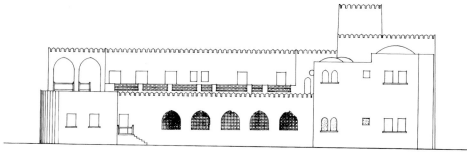

Alpha Bianca House, elevations

Nile Festival Village

1977, *designed*

Intended to occupy the majority of the Tarh al-Bahr Island in the Nile near Luxor, the design for this centre moved through three distinct phases carried out over a long period, with each scheme based on the arrival of visitors by boat at a central dock.

The first scheme, dated May 1970, divides the landing areas between the northern and southern shore of the island, bringing tourists to the centre along oblique pedestrian pathways.

The second scheme, started six years later, concentrates arrival on the southern shore only, and puts the principal guest facilities, such as the reception area, theatres, restaurants, swimming pools, and a craft *khan*, in a band spanning the entire width of the island. These public facilities displace the guest bungalows which are relocated on the periphery of the centre.

A third and final scheme, completed in March 1982, follows this second idea, accentuating the interlocking land and water at the main dock, making the entry more ceremonial and dramatic.

Akil Sami House

Dahshur 1978, *constructed*

This house, and several others that followed it in the same area, were built in local limestone because of a governmental ban on the use of mud-brick following the construction of the high dam, as well as unsatisfactory test results for the structural strength of the soil in this area, first confirmed in the Fouad Riad project. The *takhtabush* and courtyard area of the house with wooden pergola, recall the latticework notably used in the Monastirli residence in 1950.

Al-Sabah House

Kuwait 1978, *designed*

This palace for Sheikh Nasser al-Sabah was built in sand-brick, at the waterfront near Kuwait City. Perhaps more than any other residence actually completed by the architect this utilizes the courtyard typology to the fullest, using three progressively smaller gardens set in a diagonal line to chart the incremental movement through the public, semi-public and private zones of the house. A fourth court, located to offset this line, serves the library wing, and is covered by the lattice pergola shade structure first used in the Monastirli house, setting it apart from the other three, which are open.

The original design was by the architect. Omar el-Farouk, an ex-student of Fathy, was consulted on modifications to the original design. Subsequently, in mid-1986, Badi al-Abed was responsible for the completion of the house and for all the designs of woodwork, marble floors, stained glass windows, landscape around the house and all the annexes of the house.

Wadi Zarga Village

Tunisia 1978, *construction not verified*

Two-storey duplex units for this village near Tunis are carefully designed and oriented to make the best use of prevailing winds. A large claustra screen placed between each connected set of houses introduces cross-ventilation through a channel that serves both.

Alpha Bianca House

Majorca 1979, *constructed*

Built for artists Yannick Vu and Ben Jackober, this house is designed after a *ribat*, or desert fortress, with high crenellated walls, and a beautiful interior garden. The interior woodwork was executed by the al-Nagar family, who worked on many of Fathy's houses and also asked him to design a house for them on the same island.

Al-Nagar House

Majorca 1980, *construction not verified*

Designed for the family of carpenters that worked with the architect on much of his work, near Palma.

Casaroni House

Shabramant 1980, *constructed*

This is one of Fathy's stone houses in Shabramant, for Nazli and Samilha Casaroni, which they poetically called 'Mit Rehan' or 'Pathway of the Basil'. Original plans for a one-storey weekend house were changed once construction began, and a second storey added, when the clients realized the beauty of the site, which has a view of the Pyramids at Giza. A relative, Mahmud Fahmi, acted as the project manager, seeing to the rapid completion of every detail, down to the use of helba plant oil for sealing the limestone blocks to prevent discolouration. This house, which had one of the most pleasant of all garden courts of any of Fathy's projects, has now been altered.

Dar al-Islam Village
Abiquiu, New Mexico, USA 1980,
partially constructed

Dar al-Islam village was first conceived by Abdullah Nuridin Durkee, after a chance meeting with Saudi businessman Sahl Kabani on a pilgrimage to Mecca in 1979. Both men discussed the possibility of a community for American Muslims who had become cut off from the mainstream of their belief. Visualized as a religious and educational, as well as a residential centre, the community was to be a prototype for others to follow. The founders chose 1200 acres of land in the Chama river valley near Abiquiu, fifty miles north of Santa Fe, New Mexico. The land offered great potential for farming, as well as for privacy. While the village mosque has been built to his design, the remaining plan has been altered, and local building codes have made it difficult to use adobe construction.

Menia Village
1980, *construction not verified*

The proposed village was to consist of nine housing clusters, organized around individual and uniformly square central courts, and based on the clear separation of pedestrians from vehicular traffic. The two-storey high housing clusters are compact and inward-facing.

Murad Greiss House
Shabramant 1980, *constructed*

Built in white limestone, for Dr and Mrs Murad Greiss near Abu Sir. A central *qa'a* and extending *takhtabush* are used to separate a large garden, on the desert side, from a smaller one near the road.

Roxbury Mosque
Boston, USA 1980, *construction not verified*

This mosque was designed for the Muslim community in this residential district of Boston.

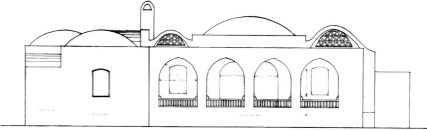

Andrioli House, elevation

Alaa al-din Mustafa House
1981, *construction not verified*

Designed for the Nubian master mason who assisted Fathy in building many of his projects, this house is a direct reinterpretation of a traditional Nubian house as found in Abu al-Riche or Gharb Aswan in Upper Egypt today, with a symbolic doorway leading directly into a series of rooms lined up on either side of a vestibule set aside for the entertainment of guests. A long, vaulted room to the left of the door has a *mastaba* or built-in seat, just as in the traditional model, for visitors, and a door at the rear of the entrance leads across a central court to the private, family area of the house. Nubian decorative motifs are used throughout.

Hatem Sadeq House
Giza 1981, *constructed*

Designed as an artist's studio, this house has not been built according to the architect's plans, which were based upon a carefully arranged series of courtyards, and a swimming pool.

Sadat Resthouse
Gharb Husayn 1981, *constructed*

Designed for the late President Anwar Sadat, as a resthouse to be used on official trips to the isolated area of Gharb Husayn, near Lake Nasser in Nubia, the residence is actually made up of three separate buildings sequentially organized according to status. The first of these is laid out like a caravanserai, for house security police and bodyguards. The second part, which is divided from the security block by a garden, is for extended family and important guests. The third was reserved for the President's family alone, and looks out over Lake Nasser.

Andrioli House
Fayyum 1984, *constructed*

Built for Gerry Andrioli near the village of Tunis al-Gabal, the house differs significantly from Fathy's plans, which called for more steeply curved dome outlines, and the partial closure of a *maqa'ad*, overlooking a palm grove, the Birkit Qarun and desert beyond.

Hasan Rashad House
Tanta 1986, *constructed*

Built in the Delta region of Egypt, this house uses local stone, and contrasts dramatically with the lush vegetation characteristic of the area.

Khalil al-Talhuni House
Jordan 1988, *constructed*

Built for a professor at Jordan University in Amman, this house is an unusually fine example of Fathy's consistent care for residential space used for hospitality. The outside area, enclosed by arcades, is primarily given over to this function, and balances well with the more private character of the interior.

Children's Hospital
Siwa 1989, *constructed*

A primary and preventative health care centre for women and children in the Siwa Oasis, Egypt, this project was commissioned by the Aga Khan Organization for Social Development.

Tilawi Residence
Kharga 1989, *constructed*

Built for the local governor of the Kharga Oasis.

Notes

Introduction

1 Taha Husayn, quoted in Jacques Berque, *Cultural Expression in Arab Society Today*, University of Texas Press, Austin, 1978, p. 33.
2 Hassan Fathy, lecture at Dar al-Islam, Abiquiu, New Mexico, June 1980 (unpublished).
3 Hassan Fathy, in interview with Yorick Blumenfeld, 'Beyond Human Scale', Architectural Association Quarterly 6, No. 3/4 1974, pp. 54.
4 Hassan Fathy, lecture at University of Essex, entitled 'The Arab House in the Urban Setting', 1970.

Chapter 1
Early Career: 1928–45

1 Undated, unpublished manuscript.
2 Interview with the author, Cairo 1986.
3 'An Ekistic Approach to the Problem of Roofing in Peasant Housing', Ministry of Scientific Research, Cairo, working paper no. 2/b, vol. 17, no. 105, June 1964, p. 393.

Chapter 2
New Gourna: 1945–47

1 *Architecture for the Poor*, University of Chicago Press, Chicago, 1973, p. 17.
2 *Ibid.*, p. 70–71.
3 *Ibid.*, p. 73.
4 In James Steele, *Hassan Fathy*, Academy Editions, London 1988, p. 167 (from previously unpublished manuscript).
5 'Mosque Architecture', undated, unpublished manuscript, p. 10.
6 *Ibid.*, p. 13.
7 'Egypte, Nouveau Village de Gourna', *L'Architecture d'Aujourd'hui* 39, no. 140, 1968, pp. 12–13.
8 *Architecture for the Poor*, p. 45.
9 Hassan Fathy, 'Gourna Village', *Atlantic Monthly*, no. 198, October 1956, p. 158.
10 'Pays d'Utopie', undated, unpublished manuscript, p. 16.
11 *L'Architecture d'Aujourd'hui* 39, no. 140, 1968, p. 16.

Chapter 3
Further Testing of New Ideas: 1948–67

1 *DA Review*, special issue on Constantinos Doxiades, July 1976, p. 12.
2 *Ibid.*, p. 2.
3 Internal memo by Hassan Fathy ('Hammams'), Doxiades Associates, 26 February 1958.
4 Internal memo by Constantinos Doxiades ('Plans for village in Mussayib by Professor Hassan Fathy'), Doxiades Associates, 21 July 1958, courtesy Athens Technological Organization.
5 *Ibid.*
6 Interview with Myrto Antonopoulou-Bogdanou, Athens, 4 June 1992.
7 Interview with John Papaioannou, Athens, 4 June 1992.
8 Interview with Nicky Coldstream, London, 15 May 1992.
9 As originally formulated, the itinerary was to include twenty cities, beginning in Cairo, moving on to Khartoum, Juba, Fort Lamy, Doula, Lagos, Kano, Porto-Novo, Lome, Abidjan, Ouagadougou, Bouake, Monrovia, Conakry, Dakar, Casablanca, Marrakech, Tunis, and Tripoli. By December political events and passport restrictions made it necessary for Fathy to alter his plans considerably, since it would have been impractical to visit Juba and Fort Lamy as well as Morocco and Tunisia, and his list diminished to a still ambitious sequence of eighteen cities. In the order visited, these were: Cairo, Khartoum, Kano, Lagos, Accra, Abidjan, Bouake, Ouagadougou, Bamako, Dakar, Conakry, Monrovia, Lome, Contonou, Porto-Novo, Douala, Yauounde, and Tripoli, returning to Cairo.
10 Hassan Fathy, 'Planning and Building in the Arab Tradition: The Village Experiment at Gourna', in *The Metropolis and the Arab World*, Monroe Berger (ed.), Allied Publishers, New York/Delhi, 1962, p. 227.
11 Lance Morrow, 'Africa: The Scramble for Existence', *Time Magazine*, 7 September 1992, p. 43.
12 Hassan Fathy, 'Le Christ Recrucifié', Doxiades Associates, 19 May 1961, courtesy Athens Technological Institute.
13 Constantinos Doxiades and John Papaioannou, *Ecumenopolis: The Inevitable City of Future*, Athens Centre of Ekistics, 1974, p. xiv, and John Papaioannou in interview, Athens, 6 June 1992.

Chapter 4
Late Career: 1967–89

1 Hassan Fathy, lecture at Dar al-Islam, Abiquiu, New Mexico, June 1980 (unpublished).

Conclusion

1 Edward W. Said, *Orientalism*, Vintage Books, New York, 1979, p. 203.
2 *Ibid.*, p. 301.
3 Conversation with Hassan Fathy, Cairo, 1988.
4 Clifford James, *The Predicament of Culture*, Harvard University Press, Cambridge, p. 265.
5 *Ibid.*, p. 265.
6 Quoted in Said, *Orientalism*, p. 35.
7 *Ibid.*, p. 87.
8 Anwar Abdel Malek, 'Orientalism in Crisis,' *Diogenes* 44, Winter 1963, p. 107–8.
9 Leandro Madrazo, 'Durand and the Science of Architecture,' *Journal of Architectural Education*, September 1994, p. 13.
10 Kenneth Frampton, *Modern Architecture 1851–1945*, Rizzoli, New York, 1981, p. 260.
11 James, *The Predicament of Culture*, p. 9.
12 See Hassan Fathy, 'The Qa'a of the Cairene Arab House.' Colloque International sur l'Histoire du Caire 1969, Proceedings, Ministry of Culture Cairo, 1972.
13 James, *The Predicament of Culture*, p. 10.

Bibliography

WRITINGS BY HASSAN FATHY

Mosque Architecture. Undated manuscript, Archives, Aga Khan Award for Architecture, Geneva

'Planning and Building in The Arab Tradition: The Village Experiment at Gourna' in Monroe Berger (ed.), *The New Metropolis and the Arab World*, Allied Publisher, New Delhi, 1964, p. 210–27

'Le Christ Recrucifié', Doxiades Associates, May 19, 1961, Courtesy Athens Technological Institute

Construire avec le Peuple: Histoire d'un Village d'Egypte, Gourna, 2 vols, Editeur Sinbad, Paris, 1977–78. Draft first published in Egypt in 1961

Gourna: A Tale of Two Villages. Ministry of Culture, Cairo, 1969, p. 295

Urban Architecture in the Middle East. Beirut Arab University, 1971 (Arabic)

The Arab House in the Urban Setting: Past, Present and Future, Longman, London, 1972 (Fourth Carreras Arab Lecture, University of Essex, 3 November 1970)

Architecture for the Poor: An Experiment in Rural Egypt. The University of Chicago Press, 1973

Architect: an Exhibition of Selected Projects (cat.). School of Architecture and Planning, MIT, Spring, 1981

Natural Energy and Vernacular Architecture. Principles and Examples with Reference to Hot Arid Climates. University of Chicago Press, 1986

Articles

'Le Nouveau Village de Gourna (Egypte)', *Architecture Française*, 8, No. 73/74, 1947, pp. 78–82

'Le Pays d'Utopie', *La Revue du Caire*, No. 24, November 1949, pp. 8–35

'La Voute dans l'Architecture Egyptienne', *La Revue du Caire*, No. 27, May 1951, pp. 14–20

'Gourna Village', *Atlantic Monthly*, No. 198, October 1956, pp. 156–57

'Hammams', internal memo, Doxiades Associates, 26 February, 1958

'Comments on the draft Dox: The Regional Plan for the Development of Greater Mussayib', internal memo, with comments by A. Hadjopoulos, Doxiades Associates, 24 June, 1958, p. 1

'Rural Self-Help Housing', *International Labor Review*, 83, 1962, pp. 1–17

With Salah Higab and Shouhri Tewfrh, 'Survey of Traditional Houses in Nubia'. Survey and measured drawings prepared for the Institute for Art and Folklore Studies, Ministry of Culture and National Orientation, Cairo, October 1962 (in Arabic)

'Planning and Building in the Arab Tradition: The Village Experiment at Gourna', *The New Metropolis and the Arab World*, Monroe Berger (ed.), 1964, pp. 211–29. Allied Publishers, New Delhi

'An Ekistic Approach to the Problem of Roofing in Peasant House-Building', Council of Building and Housing Research, Ministry of Scientific Research,

Cairo, working paper no. 2/8. Vol. 17, No. 105, June 1964, pp. 391–98

'Model Houses for El-Dareeya, Saudi Arabia', *Ekistics*, 22, No. 124, 1966, pp. 214–19

'Egypte, Nouveau Village de Gourna', *L'Architecture d'Aujourd'hui*, 39, No. 140, 1968, pp. 12–17

'The Qa'a of the Cairene Arab House. Its Development and Some New Ages for Its Design Concept', *Colloque International sur l'Histoire du Cairo*, 1969, Seminar Proceeding, Ministry of Culture, Cairo, 1972, pp. 135–52

'Constancy, Transposition and Change in the Arab City', *Medina to Metropolis*, L. Carl Brown (ed.), Darwin Press, Princeton, 1973

'The City of the Future', internal report to Athens Centre of Ekistics. (The project is also reported by C. A. Doxiades and J. G. Papaioannou in Ecumenopolis, *The Inevitable City of the Future*, W. W. Norton & Co., New York, 1974)

'Beyond the Human Scale: Hassan Fathy', interview by Yorick Blumenfeld, *Architectural Association Quarterly*, 6, 1974, pp. 53–57

'Self-Help Mud Building, Egypt', *Architectural Design*, No. 46, 1976, p. 596

Proceedings of Seminar I of Aga Khan Award for Architecture. Aiglemont, France, April 1978, published in *Toward an Architecture in the Spirit of Islam*. AKAA, 1980, p. 56

Reports for the City of the Future

R-ERES 14/20.4.61, Reports on towns visited in North and West Africa – Introduction

R-ERES 15/11.5.61, Africa – Case studies

R-ERES 15(2)/3.6.61, Africa – Omdurman, Khartoum

R-ERES 15(3)/3.6.61, Africa – Kano

R-ERES 15(5)/3.6.61, Africa – Lagos

R-ERES 15(5) was cancelled

R-ERES 15(6)/20.6.61, Africa – Abidjan

R-ERES 15(7)/3.6.61, Africa – Bouake

R-ERES 15(8)/22.6.61, Africa – Ouagadougou

R-ERES 15(9)/28.6.61, Africa – Togo

R-ERES 15(10)/2.7.61, Africa – Tripoli

R-ERES 15(11)/2.7.61, Africa – Some Conclusions

R-ERES 15 Appendix 1/30.6.61, Africa – Case studies of cities visited – The congress for cultural freedom the metropolis of the Arab world

R-ERES 24(1)/17.7.61, COF – Contribution to the final report – General Introduction

R-ERES 24(2)/1.8.61, COF – Contribution to the final report – General Introduction

R-ERES 27/18.8.61, The dwelling within the urban settlement

R-ERES 27(2)/25.8.61, Explanation of some points in R-ERES 27 (The dwelling within the urban settlement) with reference to para. 93

R-ERES 27(3)/25.8.61, The size and shape of house-plots

R-ERES 34/28.8.61, Religion and the City of the Future

R-ERES 35/1.9.61, Aesthetics in the City of the Future

R-ERES 36/5.9.61, A note on the city of tomorrow

OTHER BOOKS

Abu-Lughod, Janet L., Cairo, *1001 Years of the City Victorious*. Princeton University Press, 1971

Agarwal, Anil, *Mud, Mud: the Potential of Earth-Based Materials for Third World Housings*. Earthscan, International Institute for Environmental and Development, London, 1981

———, *Kitab al-Suluk li Marifat Duwal al-Muluk* [History of the Mamluk Sultans]. 2 vols, Dar al Kutub al-Misriyah, Cairo, 1936–58

Avennes, Emile Prisse d', *Arab Art as seen through the Monument of Cairo from the 7th to the 18th century*. Al Saqi Books, London, 1983 (first pub. Paris, 1877)

Bardet, Gaston, *Le Nouvel Urbanisme*. Edition Vincent Freal et Cie, 1948

Bell, G. and J. Tyrwhitt, (eds), *Human Identity in the Urban Environment*. Penguin Books, London, 1972

Berger, Monroe (ed), *The New Metropolis in the Arab World*. Allied Publishers, New Delhi and New York, 1964

Berque, Jacques, *Cultural Expression in Arab Society Today*. University of Texas Press, Austin, 1978

Bindel, Ernst; *Pythagoras, Leben und Lehre in Wirklichkeit und Legende*, Verlag Freies Geistesleben Stuttgart, 1962. Key reference for City of the Future report.

Bloom, Jonathan, *Minaret, Symbol of Islam*, Oxford 1989

Brace-Taylor, Brian, *Tunisia, Egypt, Morocco: Contemporary Houses Traditional Values* (exh. cat.). Zamana Gallery, London, 1985

Brunhes, Jean, *Human Geography: An Attempt at the Positive Classification*, Rand McNally and Company, Chicago and New York, 1978

Chombart de Lauwe, J., 'Problems of Agricultural Co-operation', report to the Organization for Economic Co-operation and Development, 1960. Key reference for City of the Future report.

———, *Famille et Habitation*, Centre National de la Recherche Scientifique, Paris, 1959, p. 197

Clerget, Marcel, *Le Caire*, 2 vols, Cairo, 1934

Creswell, K. A. C., *Early Muslim Architecture*. The Clarendon Press, Oxford, 2 vols, 1932 and 1940

———, *The Muslim Architecture of Egypt: Abbuyids and Early Bahrite Mamluks, AD 1171–1326*. The Clarendon Press, Oxford, 1959

———, *The Muslim Architecture of Egypt: Ikhshids and Fatimids, AD 939–1171*. Republished by Hacker Art Books, New York, 1978

Curtis, William J. R., *Modern Architecture Since 1900*. Phaidon Press, Oxford, 1982

Description de l'Egypte. 20 vols, Imprimerie nationale, Paris, 1809–13

Dethier, Jean, *Down to Earth.* Facts on File Inc., New York, 1983

Du Noy, Pierre Lecomte, *La Dignité Humaine,* La Colombe, Paris, 1948

Eddington, Arthur Stanley, *The Nature of the Physical World.* The University of Michigan Press, 1958

El-Farouk, Omar, John Norton, Wendy Etchells, Jocelyn Levaux, Allan Cain and Farroukh Ashfar, *Climatic Study of Traditional Building, Cairo.* Third World Studies Unit, Architectural Association of Architecture, London, 1973

Fry, Dabobert (ed.), *Sufism and the Islamic Tradition: The Lamahat and Sataat of Shah Waliullah.* Octagon Press, London, reprinted 1980. Key reference for City of the Future report.

Garcin, J. C., B. Maury, J. Revault and M. Zakariya, *Palais et Maisons du Caire I: Epoque Mamelouke (XIII–XVI siècles).* Editions du Centre National de la Recherche Scientifique, Paris, 1982. Insight into Fatimid Mamluk typologies used by Fathy.

Golany, Gideon, *Architecture in the Arid Zone.* Architectural Press, London, 1982

Hardy, George, *L'Art Negre: L'Art Animiste des Noirs d'Afrique.* Henri Laurens, Tournon, 1927, pp. 1–7

Hawkes, Jacquetta, *The Atlas of Early Man.* St Martins Press, New York, 1976

Hoag, John D. *Islamic Architecture.* Harry N. Abrams, Inc., New York, 1977

Jackson, Sir Thomas Graham, *Byzantine and Romanesque Architecture.* Cambridge University Press, 1913 (1st edn) and 1920 (2nd edn). Reprinted by Hacker Art Books, New York, 1975

Jairazbhoy, R. A., *Outline of Islamic Architecture.* Asia Publishing House, Inc., New York, 1972

Japp, Francis R., *Inorganic Chemistry,* LCA Brothers and Co., Philadelphia, 1885

Kazantzakis, Nikos, *Christ Recrucified,* Faber and Faber, London and Boston, 1954, esp. Chapter VII, 'God is a Potter: He Works in Mud', p. 168–92

Khalili, N., *Geltafan Earth: a Revolution in the Traditional Architecture of Iran.* Museum of Contemporary Arts, Tehran, 1980

Kramrisch, Stella, *The Hindu Temple,* University of Calcutta, Vol. I, 1946. Key reference for City of the Future report.

Lane, Edward William, *Egypt,* British Museum, London, MS no. 34.080
———, *The Manners and Customs of the Modern Egyptians,* London, 1836. Reprinted by Everyman Library, c. 1908

Lloyd, Seton, *The Archaeology of Mesopotamia* (rev. edn), Thames and Hudson, London, 1984

Lubicz, R. A. Schwaller de, *Le Temple dans l'Homme, Tome I. Collection Architecture et Symboles Sacres.* Dervy-Livres, Paris, 1985

Al-Magrizi, Taqi al-Din Ahmad, *Al-Mawa iz wa al-Itibar fi Dhikr al-Khitat wa al-Athar* [Lessons and Considerations in Knowing the Structure of Countries (Cities)]. 2 vols, Bulag Press, Cairo, 1853

Maroon, Fred J. and P. H. Newby, *The Egypt Story: Its Art, Its Monuments, Its People, Its History,* Chanticleer Press, New York

Maury, Bernard, *Palais et Maisons du Caire,* 11, Epoque Ottomane. Paris, 1983

McHenry, Paul Graham, Jr. *Adobe and Rammed Earth Buildings: Design and Construction,* Wiley Interscience, New York, 1983

Michell, George (ed.), *Architecture of the Islamic World,* Thames and Hudson, London, 1978 (reprinted 1984)

Olgyay, Victor, *Design With Climate: Bioclimatic Approach to Architectural Regionalism.* Princeton University Press, Princeton, 1963

Papadopoulo, Alexander, *Islam and Muslim Art.* Thames and Hudson, London, 1980, p. 40

Paraf, Pierre, *Anthologie du romantisme.* Albin Michel Editeur, Paris, 1927. Key reference for City of the Future report.

Parker, Richard B. and Sabin, Robin, *A Practical Guide to Islamic Monuments in Cairo,* The American University in Cairo Press, 1974

Patai, Raphael, *The Arab Mind,* Charles Scribner's Sons, New York, 1983

Pauty, E., *Les Palais et les Maisons de l'Epoque musulmane au Caire,* Imprimerie de l'Institut Français d'Archeologie Orientale, Paris, 1932

Petruccioli, Attilio, *Hassan Fathy, Architectura nei Paesi Islamici,* Seconda Mostra Internazionale di Architettura, Edizioni La Biennale Di Venezia, 1982

'Places of Public Gathering in Islam', Proceedings of Seminar Five, Architectural Transformation in the Islamic World, Amman, Jordan, May 4–7, 1980, Aga Khan Award for Architecture

Raymond, André, *The Great Arab Cities in the 16th to the 18th Centuries – An Introduction,* New York University Press, 1984

Richards, J. M., I. Serageldin, Darl Rastorfer, *Hassan Fathy.* Mimar Books, Concept Media, Singapore, 1985

Russell, Dorothea, *Medieval Cairo and the Monasteries of the Wadi Natrun.* Weidenfeld and Nicholson, London, 1962

Al-Sayyad, Nezar, *Streets of Islamic Cairo – A Configuration of Urban Themes and Patterns.* The Aga Khan Programs for Islamic Architecture, Harvard University and MIT Studies in Islamic Architecture, No. 2, 1981

Schuon, Frithjof, *Understanding Islam.* Mandala Books, Unwin Paperbacks, London, 1981, p. 35

Seton-Williams, Veronica and Peter Stocks, *Blue Guide Egypt.* Ernest Benn, London, 1983

Smith, E. Baldwin, *The Dome: A Study in the History of Ideas.* Princeton, 1978

Souvaget, Jean, *Introduction to the History of Muslim East..* University of California Press, 1965

Talbot Rice, David, *Islamic Art.* Thames and Hudson, London, 1965

Thompson, Darcy Wentworth, *On Growth and Form.* The University Press, Cambridge, 1942

US Department of Housing and Urban Development, Office of International Affairs, *Mud Brick Roofs.* No. 42, Washington, D.C., 1957

Woytinsky, W. S. and E. S., *India: The Awakening Giant,* Harper & Brothers, New York, 1957
———, *World Population and Production, Trends and Outlooks,* The Twentieth Century Fund, New York, 1953

Wik, Tina, *Hassan Fathy arkitekt I tredje varlden,* Etnografiska Museet, Stockholm, 1986

Wittkower, Rudolf, *Architectural Principles in the Age of Humanism,* W. W. Norton & Company Inc., New York, 1971

Articles and Essays

Abel, Chris, 'Regional Tranformation', *The Architectural Review,* Vol. CLXXX. No. 1077, November 1986

Asfour, Farroukh, 'Hassan Fathy: Social Visionary or Architectural Aesthete?', *Mimar,* Architecture in Development, No. 20, April–June 1986

Agarwal, Anil, 'Research: Mud as a Traditional Building Material', *The Changing Rural Habitat,* Aga Khan Award for Architecture, Vol. I, 1982, pp. 139–46

El-Araby, K. M. G., 'Fathy, H.: Gourna: a Tale of Two Villages' (review), *Journal of the American Institute of Planners.* No. 38, May 1972, pp. 190–91

'An Introduction to Islamic Architecture', *UIA International Architect,* Issue 7, 1985, London

'Architectural Transformation in the Islamic World', proceedings of Seminar Nine, 'The Expanding Metropolis: Coping with the Urban Growth of Cairo', Cairo, 1984, Aga Khan Award for Architecture, Concept Media

Bloom, Jonathan, 'Five Fatimid Minarets in Upper Egypt', *Journal of the Society of Architectural Historians,* XLIII, pp. 162–67, May 1984

Clark, Felicia, 'Appropriate Invention' (review of *Architecture for the Poor*), *Architectural Record,* 168, January 1980, p. 187

Cliff, Ursula, 'Designers of Human Settlements. Hassan Fathy', *Design and Environment,* No. 7, Spring 1967, pp. 22–25

Cousin, Jean-Pierre, 'Hassan Fathy', *L'Architecture d'Aujourd'hui,* No. 195, February 1978, pp. 42–78

Danby, Miles, 'The Islamic Architectural Tradition and the House', proceedings of symposium at KFU, Dammam, 1983

Dethier, Jean, 'On Architecture in Unbaked Earth', *Urbanisme Architecture,* No. 7, Centre Georges Pompidou, Paris, 1981

Dillon, David, 'A Mosque for Abiquiu', *Progressive Architecture,* June 1983, pp. 90–92

Dryansky, G. Y., 'Ninety-Four Doors: Hispano-Mooresque House on the Isle of Majorca', *Architectural Digest,* August 1985, pp. 120–25

Doxiades, Constantinos and John Papaioannou, 'Ecumenopolis, the Inevitable City of the Future', Athens Centre of Ekistics, 1974, p. XIV

Dunham, Daniel, 'The Courtyard House as a Temperature Regulator', *New Scientist*, 8 September, 1960, pp. 663–66. Study of central courtyards to which Fathy frequently referred.

Durkee, Abdullah Nuridin, 'Hassan Fathy in New Mexico', *Via. 7*, Paula Behrens and Anthony Fisher (eds), *Architectural Journal of the Graduate School of Fine Arts*, University of Pennsylvania and the MIT Press, 1980, pp. 58–75

———, 'Qariyat Muslimah in New Mexico', *Al-Majal*, December 1981

Friedlander, Shems, 'The Dream of Hassan Fathy', *Geo*, Vol. 3, December 1981, pp. 91–99

———, 'In Touch with the Earth', *Portfolio*, May/June 1982, pp. 106–9

———, 'Hassan Fathy: A Voyage to New Mexico', *Arts in the Islamic World*, Vol. 1, p. 1, Winter 1982/83, pp. 31–35, Islamic Arts Foundation, London

Grabar, Oleg, 'The Architecture of the Middle Eastern City from Past to Present: The Case of the Mosque', *Middle Eastern Cities*. Berkeley, 1969, pp. 26–46

Graham, John, 'Coptic Coexistence', *UIA International Architect*, Issue 7, p. 32

Haswell, C. J., 'Cairo, Origin and Development: Some Notes on the Influence of the River Nile and Its Changes', *Bulletin de la Société Royale de Géographie d'Egypte*, 3 and 4, 1922, p. 18

Holod, Renata and Darl Rastorfer, 'Hassan Fathy, Chairman's Award', *Architecture and Community Building in the Islamic World Today*, 1983, pp. 235–45, New York

Homans, Rich, 'Hassan Fathy', *Adobe Today*, No. 29

———, 'How the Builders of Rosso Raised a Miracle from the Mud', *South*, July 1983

Ibrahim, Saad-Eddin, 'Cairo: A Sociological Profile', proceedings of Seminar Nine 'The Expanding Metropolis: Coping with the Urban Growth of Cairo', Cairo, November 11–15, 1984, Aga Khan Award for Architecture, Concept Media

King, Geoffrey, 'Architectural Traditions and Decoration in Central and Eastern Arabia', *The Arab City*, seminar proceedings, Medina, 1981

Lobell, Mimi, '*Architecture for the Poor* by Hassan Fathy' (review), *East West Journal*, June 1976, pp. 52–53

MacFarquar, Neil, 'Mud Brick', Arts in the Islamic World, Vol. 2, No. 2, Summer 1984

Marquis, Robert B., 'Egypt's Prophet of Appropriate Technology, *AIA Journal*, December 1980

Massignon, Louis, 'Les corps de métiers et la cité Islamique', *Revue Internationale de Sociologie*, Vol. 28, 1920, pp. 473–89

Monroe, Peter, 'A Place for Prayer', *Arts in the Islamic World*, Vol. 3, No. 2, Summer 1985

Morrow, Lance, 'Africa: The Scramble for Existence', *Time Magazine*, 'The Agony of Africa', September 7, 1992, p. 34

Mourad, Moustafa, 'Egypt: Policies and Politics', *The Architectural Review*, Vol. CLXXVII, No. 1062, August 1985

Moustaader, Attilio, 'Gourna: the Dream Continued', *Mimar*, 16, April–June 1985, Concept Media, Singapore, pp. 54–59

Petruccioli, Attilio, 'Tracking Down the Poet of Raw Bricks', *Spazio Societa*, 5, 1982, pp. 42–61

'Plans for village in Mussayib by Professor Hassan Fathy', internal memo of Doxiades Associates by Constantinos Doxiades, 21 July 1958, courtesy Athens Technological Organization

Prussin, Isabelle, '*Architecture for the Poor* by Hassan Fathy' (review), *Journal of the Society of Architectural Historians*, 37, March 1978, p. 55

Raymond, André, 'Essai de geographique des quartiers de residence aristocratique au Caire au XVIIIème siècle, *Journal of the Economic and Social History of the Orient*, Vol. VI, Part 1, May 1936, pp. 58–103

———, 'The Residential District of Cairo During the Ottoman Period', *The Arab City*, Proceedings of a Symposium, Medina, 1981

Richards, J. M., 'Gourna: a Lesson in Basic Architecture', *Architectural Review*, 147, February 1970, pp. 109–18

Scanlon, George, 'Preliminary Report: Excavations at Fustat, 1964', *Journal of the American Research Center in Egypt*, VI, 1965, pp. 7–30

Schilling, Jacob, 'Gourna: ein Architektonisches Experiment in Ägypten', *Deutsche Bauzeitung*, 70, January 1965, pp. 46–50

Schleifer, S. Abdullah, 'Hassan Fathy's Abiquiu: An Experimental Islamic Education Center in Rural New Mexico', *Ekistics*, 302, January/February 1984, pp. 56–60

———, 'Hassan Fathy: A Voyage to New Mexico', *Arts in the Islamic World*, Vol. 1, No. 1, Winter 1982–83

———, 'Islamic Architecture and the Discipline of Design: The Work of Omar El-Farouk', *Arts in the Islamic World*, Vol. 2, no. 2, summer 1984

Seamon, Davis, 'Heidegger's Notion of Dwelling and One Concrete Interpretation as Indicated by Hassan Fathy's Architecture for the Poor', *Geoscience & Man*, Vol. 24, 30 April 1984, pp. 43–53

Serageldin, Mona, 'Planning for New Nubia 1960–80', *The Changing Rural Habitat*, Vol. 1, Concept Media, Singapore, 1982

Shahed, Saleem, 'Abdel Wahed El-Wakil: Interpreter of a Living Tradition', *Arts in the Islamic World*, Vol. 1, No. 4, Winter 1983–84

Sugich, Haroon, 'Traditional Architecture Finds a Royal Patron', *Arts in the Islamic World*. Vol. 3, No. 4, Winter 1985–86, p. 47

———, 'Mosques Should Reflect the Highest Form of Architecture: Wakil', *Arab News,* 26 September, 1985

Swan, Simone, 'Hassan Fathy Demonstrates Ancient Construction Methods in New Mexico', *Architectural Record*, 168, December 1980, p. 39

Toulan, Nohad A., 'Climatic Considerations in the Design of Urban Housing in Egypt', *Housing in Arid Lands*, Architectural Press, London, 1980

Toynbee, A., L. Munford, H. Fathy, B. Fuller, C. Doxiades, C. Correa, P. Mwaluko,

R. McNamara, J. F. C. Turner, 'Designers of Human Settlements: Nine Men, Architects, Historians and Bureaucrats Who Help to Shape Cities', *Design and Environment* , no. 25, 1976, pp. 18–25

Vaughan, Joe, 'Hassan Fathy', *Adobe Today*, No. 30, pp. 29–31

El-Wakil, Abdel Wahed, 'Architecture, Identity and Tradition', *Al-Benaa*, 25, Moharram-Safar 1406, pp. 65–75

Ward, Colin, 'For the Fellah with Nothing', *Royal Institute of British Architects Journal*, 81, February 1974, pp. 35–36

Audio and Video Cassettes

'Architect Hassan Fathy', produced by A. S. Kington, NASS Ltd., 49 Goodge St., London

'Hassan Fathy Lecture, Abiquiu, New Mexico, 1980', 1. Tape 4, side A and B; 2. Tape 6, side A and B; 3. Tape 7, side A. Transcriptions by J. Palkovic, courtesy of the Aga Khan Award for Architecture

'Roofs Under Foot: The Adobe Barrel Vault', produced by Bill White, Blanco, Texas

VCR News Coverage of Fathy's Visit to Abiquiu, KGGM-TV, CBS Albuquerque Affiliate, Charles Shipley, reporter

Glossary

Abbasid dynasty descended from Abbas, ruled Egypt 750–868
badana family group within a tribe
baratsi lightweight roof truss constructed as a folded slab from woven wire, reeds and cement
bayt palace
caravanserai inn with large inner court
claustra pierced dividing wall
dahliz antechamber
diwan sitting room
diwan hasil sitting room reserved for women
durqa'a central space of the **qa'a**
Fatimid descended from Fatima, daughter of Muhammad; dynasty ruled Egypt 969–1171
feddan measure of land equivalent to approx. 1 acre (0.405 hectare)
gama'a congregational mosque
haj pilgrimage, especially to Mecca
hammam public bath
haram private quarters of a house or sanctuary of a mosque

iwan ancillary space, often adjoining **qa'a**
kamariyya stained-glass windows joined with plaster
khan accommodation for travellers
khayma flat-roofed loggia
madrasa Islamic school, often attached to mosque
magaz indirect or offset entry
maghribi North African horseshoe arch
majlis reception hall for male guests
malkaf wind catch
Mamluk dynasty, ruled Egypt 1250–1517
mandara guest sitting room
manzil large house
maqa'ad loggia, open 'room'
mastaba step or bench
mojabab see **magaz**
muallim benna master mason
muqarnas honeycomb vaulting
mashrabiya screen or grille of turned wood
palestra public area for teaching or display of wrestling, etc.

qa'a main hall of a house, comprising a **durqa'a** and two **iwans**, usually reserved solely for male guests
qibla direction of prayer
qubba dome; (by extension) tomb
ribat fortified monastery
riwaq portico; living quarters for teachers
salamlik pavilion
salsabil water-fed cooling plate, usually of marble, used in conjunction with a **malkaf**
Sassanian dynasty descended from Sasan, which ruled the Persian Empire 224–651
shukshaykha vented or fenestrated lantern of a dome
suq open-air market
squinch arch-shaped element spanning a corner, resolving square supporting walls with the circular base of a dome through an 8- then 16-sided transitional zone
takhtabush covered outdoor sitting area between two courtyards
umriyad coloured glass inserted in a dome

Acknowledgments

The Aga Khan Award for Architecture has contributed generously from their extensive archive on Hassan Fathy to make this publication possible and the publisher and author gratefully acknowledge their kind support.

I would like to thank Jo Newson for encouraging me to proceed with this project and for moral support during completion. I also appreciate the co-operation of the Athens Technological Institute for whom the City of the Future project was originally prepared. Panagis Psomopoulos and John Papaioannou have been of incalculable assistance in helping to bring back to life the five-year period that Fathy was in Athens and in providing many specific leads and valuable suggestions for me to follow. Myrto Antonopoulou-Bogdanou, who worked with Fathy on the Iraq Housing Project and later became manager of the City of the Future initiative, also helped a great deal in reconstructing Fathy's responsibilities and activities during this time. George Katsoufis and Jesse Spynoy were also helpful to me in Athens.

I would also like to thank Nicola Coldstream for information about her mother, Marion Carr; Jiyada Hassanein for information about her aunt, Fathy's wife; Mona Monastirli for family documentation; Abdel Wahed el-Wakil, Omar el-Farouk and Rami Dahan for copious background research.

All illustrations appear courtesy of the author, with the following exceptions:
Title page Hassia **7** (*ar*) A. W. el-Wakil; (*br*) D. Gale **8** AKAA **10** H. Fathy **11, 13** Al-Ahram **14** AKAA **15** A. W. el-Wakil **18** (*al*) R. Dahan; (*ar*) C. Avedissian, AKAA; (*bl*) R. Dahan **19** (*bl*) C. Avedessian, AKAA **21** T. Wik **22** Gouache, 29.2 x 27 cm., courtesy AKAA **29** M. Greiss **31** R. Dahan **34** Gouache, 70.6 x 52.2 cm., AKAA **40, 41** H. Fathy **42** Gouache, 50.6 x 71 cm., AKAA **44, 46, 47** R. Dahan **48, 49** H. Fathy **52, 53** Gouache (*l*), 46.2 x 59.5 cm., AKAA; gouache (*r*), 42 x 53 cm., AKAA **55** H. Fathy **56, 57** A. W. el-Wakil **59** T. Wik **60** Gouache, 46.8 x 58 cm., AKAA **63** H. Fathy **69** Gouache, 52.8 x 45.2 cm., AKAA **70** H. Fathy **74, 75**

T. Wik **76** Gouache, 101 x 49.2 cm., AKAA **77** (*b*) A. W. el-Wakil **78** H. Fathy **82** Gouache, 47 x 60.5 cm., AKAA **84** A. W. el-Wakil **87** Gouache, 64.3 x 50.2 cm., AKAA **90, 94, 95** Casey Steele **96, 97** H. Fathy **98, 99** AKAA **100** (*a*) T. Wik, (*b*) M. Monastirli **101** H. Fathy **102** (*a*) A. W. el-Wakil **102** (*b*), **103** H. Fathy **104** (*a*) T. Wik; (*b*) R. Dahan **106** Christopher Steele **108** T. Wik **110** Doxiades Associates **115, 116, 118** AKAA **124** C. Avedissian, AKAA **126** AKAA **128** Gouache, 71.5 x 51.5 cm., AKAA **129** O. el-Farouk **130** H. Fathy **134** T. Wik **135** AKAA **136** C. Avedissian, AKAA **137** (*a*) R. Dahan; (*b*) T. Wik **138** AKAA **139** R. Dahan **140, 141** (*b*) C. Avedissian, AKAA **141** (*a*) T. Wik **142** H. Fathy **143** T. Wik **144, 145** C. Avedissian, AKAA **150, 151** AKAA **154** R. Dahan **155, 156** A. W. el-Wakil **157** Nawal Hassan **158, 164, 165, 168, 169** H. Fathy **171** (*b*) Akil Sami, AKAA **172** AKAA **174** (*b*) C. Avedissian, AKAA **175** (*a*) R. Badran **176** O. el-Farouk **177** R. Dahan **178** AKAA **Chronology** all AKAA

Index

Illustrations are indicated in *italic*. Projects are entered according to the first word of their titles in the Chronology (e.g., Fouad Riad House under F) unless marked otherwise.